THE POEM I TURN TO

ACTORS & DIRECTORS PRESENT POETRY THAT INSPIRES THEM

PREFACE BY BILLY COLLINS

AFTERWORD BY JOHN LITHGOW

EDITED BY JASON SHINDER

ADVISORY EDITORS:

MICHAEL O'KEEFE AND LILI TAYLOR

in association with the David Coleman Dukes Memorial Theatre
Scholarship Fund at the University of Southern California

sourcebooks
mediaFusion

An Imprint of
Sourcebooks, Inc.©
Naperville, Illinois

Contributor photos courtesy of: Adam Arkin (Adam Arkin), Moses Berkson (Jon Robin Baitz), Bob
Balaban (Bob Balaban), Ken Brecher (Ken Brecher), Steve Buscemi (Steve Buscemi), Brian Cox
(Brian Cox), Peter Coyote (Peter Coyote), Eve Ensler (Eve Ensler), Deborah Dobson Bach at ITHA-
CA Films (Michael Fitzgerald), Rodrigo Garcia (Rodrigo Garcia), John Robert Williams (Kathleen
Glynn), Jeff Lipsky (Daryl Hannah), Philip Seymour Hoffman (Philip Seymour Hoffman), Thomas
Duffe (Stacy Keach), Swoosie Kurtz (Swoosie Kurtz), Peter Suschitzky (Alix Lambert), Suzanne Arkin
(John Landis), John Lithgow (John Lithgow), Getty Images (Billy Luther), Matthew Maher
(Matthew Maher), Davidson & Choy Publicity (Carol Muske-Dukes, David Dukes, John Lithgow),
Mark Murray (Michael O'Keefe), Brad Fowler, 2008 (Jason Shinder), Warren Etheredge, The Warren
Report, (Stewart Stern), Holland Taylor (Holland Taylor), Stanley Tucci (Stanley Tucci), Patrick
Shepard (Taika Waititi).

All others copyright The Associated Press.

Audio produced by Diane Scanlon. Executive Producer, Jason Shinder.
Sourcebooks and the colophon are registered trademarks of Sourcebooks, Inc.

Published by Sourcebooks MediaFusion, an imprint of Sourcebooks, Inc.
P.O. Box 4410, Naperville, Illinois 60567-4410
(630) 961-3900
Fax: (630) 961-2168
www.sourcebooks.com

Library of Congress Cataloging-in-Publication Data

The poem I turn to: actors and directors present poems that inspire them / preface by Billy Collins;
afterword by John Lithgow; edited by Jason Shinder, with Michael O'Keefe and Lili Taylor.
     p. cm.
"In association with the David Coleman Dukes Memorial Theatre Scholarship Fund".
Includes index.
ISBN-13: 978-1-4022-0502-6
ISBN-10: 1-4022-0502-3
 1. Poetry--Collections. 2. Poetry--Translations into English. 3. English poetry. 4. American poetry.
I. Shinder, Jason. II. O'Keefe, Michael. III. Taylor, Lili.

PN6101.P488 2008
808.81--dc22

                          2007049737

Printed and bound in the United States of America.
       WOZ 10 9 8 7 6 5 4 3 2 1

CONTENTS

Swoosie Kurtz

Michael Lally

Alix Lambert

John Landis

Melissa Leo

John Lithgow

Billy Luther

Peter MacNicol

Matthew Maher

Walter Mosley

In the year 1887, the idea occurred to me that it was possible to devise an instrument which should do for the eye what the phonograph does for the ear, and then by the combination of the two, all motion and sound could be recorded and produced simultaneously. . . . Inventors must be poets so they may have imagination.

THOMAS A. EDISON

in memory of David Coleman Dukes
and Liam Rector

What thou lovest well remains,

                   the rest is dross

What thou lov'st well shall not be reft from thee

What thou lov'st well is thy true heritage

EZRA POUND

 TRACK 1

PREFACE

by Billy Collins, United States Poet Laureate, 2001–2003

The book you hold in your hands arose from the match-making efforts of its editor, poet Jason Shinder, who called on a number of people involved in film-making to reveal their love for—even their reliance on—a favorite poem or two. The result is both a handy anthology of poems—some well-known, others less familiar—and a set of revealing connections between certain celebrities—mostly familiar—and a few of the poems they hold dear.

Of course, there was another way of going about this, which would have been to let the poems choose their readers. That would have been my approach. Just release the writers, dead or alive, at the corner of Hollywood and Vine and see which actors and directors they would look for. I can see Neruda searching for Daryl Hannah on a sunny morning, a row of tall palms in the background. And there's Mary Oliver stopping to buy a map to the homes of the stars before paying her visits to Steve Buscemi and Stanley Tucci. Imagine Keats showing up on the doorstep of John Lithgow, or Shakespeare with a sonnet in his hand waiting on Stacy Keach's lawn—all of them believing, as many people do, that you don't choose your favorite poets, they choose you. Slowly, slowly, Sylvia Plath turns to Dianne Wiest, Heaney to Guilfoyle, lower-case Cummings to Fisher.

But taking this book for what it is, let us stop for a moment at the title, because "turn to" is a revealing verb with which to connect reader and poem. It implies that turning to a poem means more than simply facing it or giving it your attention. You turn to a poem for something. Consolation, reassurance, hope, affirmation—whatever that something might be, poetry is happy to offer it. So we like to think.

In the aftermath of the spectacular collapse of the twin towers on September 11, 2001, the act of turning to poetry enjoyed a revival. In the days and months that followed, when American flags were flying from car antennas, poems could be heard on the radio and seen featured on the op-ed pages of newspapers. The notes and spaces of what became the poem of the moment, W.H. Auden's "September 1, 1939," filled the airwaves. It seemed as if we believed that a poem could somehow make matters better, that just a few dozen words arranged in lines could help. Many American poets were asked to pull out of their pockets an appropriate poem by their own or another's hand that could be read publicly, a poem to ease the confusion, a poem to act as a stabilizing rudder to a national consciousness set adrift by an historic shock. Of all the arts, it seemed to go without saying that poetry, largely ignored in everyday American life, was the thing to "turn to." No one was heard to say: "Our nation has suffered a horrible wound: let's get tickets to the opera" or "I know how we should respond to this unprecedented, cataclysmic event: we'll go to the movies."

In times of crisis, poems, not paintings or ballet, are what people habitually reach for. Conveniently enough, poetry is always right there on the shelf waiting to be read. And the formalized language of poetry can ritualize experience and provide emotional focus. Poetry is thus seen as a kind of floatation device for those who find themselves at sea on troubled waters.

Poetry also can assure us that we are not alone; others, some of them long dead, have felt what we are feeling. They have heard the same sea, watched the same sky, looked up to see the same moon.

Besides connecting us to the past, this particular collection of poems also brings us into the company of fellow readers, specifically readers whom most of us know only from the context of the dramatic arts. By reading or re-reading these poems in the light of those who have selected them, we are admitted for a moment into the sensibility of a celebrity, which someone once defined as "a total stranger we feel we know." That Holland Taylor has a fondness for Wilfred Owen gives me a discrete insight into her taste and thinking. Until now, I had not heard the names of Jane Fonda and Rilke mentioned in the same breath. And I feel a subtle kinship with Philip Seymour Hoffman now that I know he takes delight, as I do, in Meghan O'Rourke.

Finally, in a time when the audience for poetry seems largely composed of other poets, it is encouraging to see that poetry is alive in the lives of non-practitioners, whether they are film stars or lawyers or mechanics.

So, let us forsake the supermarket glossies that tell us—or worse, show us—how much weight a film star has lost or gained. Let us dig into *The Poem I Turn To* for a rich array of poems and for a glimpse into the literary lives of the stars, the lines they turn to when they are far from the camera and crowd, alone with the page.

INTRODUCTION

A few years ago in Provo, Utah, Ken Brecher, the Executive Director of Sundance Institute, introduced me to a young woman. She had just arrived at the Sundance Institute's summer labs dedicated to supporting directors, writers, and other filmmakers in the making of new, independent films. She was an actress, Ken said. "Well, not always…" she said.

I, Ken told her, was the Director of the Institute's new Arts Writing Program, and wrote poetry. Well, not always, I wanted to say. I immediately felt an uncomfortable need to explain myself, and further, perhaps apologize for what I imagined would be the discomfort caused by that word poetry.

What, though, would that discomfort actually be about? In part, no doubt, the familiar guilt by association with the word "poetry;" that is, with the very sensitive, sad, or mad, addicted and/or heart-broken souls who write it – the doomed love story of John Keats meets the dramatic suicide of Sylvia Plath mixed up with the drug and rebellious journey of Allen Ginsberg.

It was also, in part, my discomfort, stemming from the prejudiced assumption that a busy actress, of course, would have no real interest in or understanding of poetry. And, if she did (my sanctimony persisted) it could never, of course, be as devoted and important as mine.

"Oh," she said, however, "I love to turn to poems." That was all I needed to jolt me off the murky path of misperception on which it was possible to believe an actress and a poet were living on distant continents in regard to the appreciation of poetry. What I discovered (which was already obvious to others) was that a good actor (or, for that matter, any good, fortunate human) was, of course, always shifting and changing and searching, and this uncertain and fraught state of the necessarily never satisfied is nourished and renewed, perhaps unlike anywhere else on the globe, in good poems.

The public has many fixed ideas about an actor or director, of which the most dangerous may be the imagined transforming power and luxury of fame and success. Yet the person behind the public recognition and success knows he or she must keep pursuing and reaching for a certain kind of failure – a kind of defeat that connects one with the dignity (and joy) of loneliness, fear, and uncertainty.

These essential, often contradictory, states of being, which are necessary for the good actor to sustain his or her ongoing vulnerability and capacity for empathy, are perhaps nowhere more illuminated and lucid than in the often highly distilled (and, yes, accessible) art of poetry.

I am sure that envy also played a part in my thinking the actress I met was at odds with poetry. Envy, because of the "rich" lifestyle, real and imagined, I thought she lived; envy, because it is sometimes difficult to deal with those who we think are more distinguished than us, and, in the case of movie stars, perhaps than anyone else. What I originally believed distinguished me was my (vain) claim to the special interiority and emotional sensitivity in which I believed poetry was produced. Without such a claim, there was only the poem, and its pleasure, beauty, and silence to deal with – and we were all (even actors and other non-poets) its sons and daughters.

This anthology, the first of its kind, includes the poems that many of our most distinguished actors, directors, and other movie-makers turn to. The lyrical tenderness of a poem, the physicality and beauty of the body, the passing of time, the intense sorrow of war, the great joy of nature, the elusive and ephemeral light and darkness of memory, the capacity and courage to sustain love – these are just some of the reasons why the book's contributors turn to poems.

Some contributors could not decide which two poems, of the many poems in their lives, to include. Many of the contributors knew right away. For most of the contributors, the poems they turn to live in their body, mind, and spirit, and those poems surface at will, without an instant's warning, while talking to a friend, looking out the window, or buttoning a shirt. Somehow, by this repetition, they become a kind of company and presence that stays with, comforts, and informs the contributors and who they wish, or need, to be. Their choices in this book are, then, a new and exciting poetic witness of their lives as actors, as persons, and of the times in which we work and live.

And by situating the individual private space of poetry in the social, collaborative landscape of movies, the contributors open up, challenge, and confirm the ways both arts, at their best, reach for some accuracy and truth to life. For the contributors in this book, and for so many others of all professions, both poets and movie-makers offer a language to dwell in, a gift so expressive, courageous, and honest, that at times it seems our own invention. I often think of poetic or cinematic thoughts, lines, or images for so long I come to believe they are almost my own.

But there's more.

By sharing the poems they turn to, and commenting on their choices, the contributors in this book offer testimony to our essential human need for contemplation in a world in which the velocity and volume of experience are often overwhelming. And the resistance to the speeded-up passing of time that poems represent; the need to keep what matters most about being alive going on after the movie is over, is made possible—for contributor and reader alike—by turning to the sustained intimacy and beautiful construct of a poem heard out loud, or (now) in your hands.

Jason Shinder

This book is dedicated, in part, to the memory of the actor David Coleman Dukes. Poetry was always a gift of his friendship and company, and his remarkable presence and participation as an actor and appreciator of poetry helped trigger the genesis of this book. Proceeds will support The David Coleman Dukes Memorial Theatre Scholarship Fund at the University of Southern California.

ADAM
ARKIN

TRACKS 2,3

The Waking

THEODORE ROETHKE

I wake to sleep, and take my waking slow.
I feel my fate in what I cannot fear.
I learn by going where I have to go.

We think by feeling. What is there to know?
I hear my being dance from ear to ear.
I wake to sleep, and take my waking slow.

Of those so close beside me, which are you?
God bless the Ground! I shall walk softly there,
And learn by going where I have to go.

Light takes the Tree; but who can tell us how?
The lowly worm climbs up a winding stair;
I wake to sleep, and take my waking slow.

Great Nature has another thing to do
To you and me; so take the lively air,
And, lovely, learn by going where to go.

This shaking keeps me steady. I should know.
What falls away is always. And is near.
I wake to sleep, and take my waking slow.
I learn by going where I have to go.

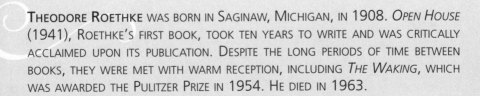

THEODORE ROETHKE WAS BORN IN SAGINAW, MICHIGAN, IN 1908. *OPEN HOUSE* (1941), ROETHKE'S FIRST BOOK, TOOK TEN YEARS TO WRITE AND WAS CRITICALLY ACCLAIMED UPON ITS PUBLICATION. DESPITE THE LONG PERIODS OF TIME BETWEEN BOOKS, THEY WERE MET WITH WARM RECEPTION, INCLUDING *THE WAKING*, WHICH WAS AWARDED THE PULITZER PRIZE IN 1954. HE DIED IN 1963.

All Night I Could Not Sleep

LI YI
Translated by Arthur Waley

All night I could not sleep
because of the moonlight on my bed.
I kept on hearing a voice calling:
Out of Nowhere, Nothing answered "yes."

LI YI WAS A CHINESE WRITER AND POET OF THE SONG DYNASTY, REGARDED BY MANY AS THE PREMIER WOMAN POET IN THE CHINESE LANGUAGE. BORN IN LICHENG IN 1084 TO A FAMILY OF OFFICIALS AND SCHOLARS, HER POETRY WAS WELL KNOWN WITHIN ELITE CIRCLES. ONLY AROUND A HUNDRED OF HER POEMS ARE KNOWN TO SURVIVE, TRACING HER VARYING FORTUNES IN LIFE.

I never know, consciously, what first draws me to a poem. It usually resonates in some way as something familiar but previously murky or obscure within me which the poem somehow crystallizes and makes more clear. THE WAKING was like that for me. I keep returning to it in this truly brilliant anthology THE RAG AND BONE SHOP OF THE HEART (edited by Robert Bly), and it speaks to me every time I read it. It's simple and quite dense at the same time, and it has a beautiful rhythm to it. It deals with themes that are more and more important with the passage of time; acceptance, intuition—stuff like that. And it manages to be simultaneously comforting and mysterious.

ALL NIGHT I COULD NOT SLEEP covers some of the same territory in a very compact way. They really complement each other, even in their titles, though I never picked them with that in mind.

-Adam Arkin

ALAN
ARKIN

The Guest House

RUMI
TRANSLATED BY COLEMAN BARKS

This being human is a guest house.
Every morning a new arrival.

A joy, a depression, a meanness,
some momentary awareness comes
as an unexpected visitor.

Welcome and entertain them all!
Even if they're a crowd of sorrows,
who violently sweep your house
empty of its furniture,
still, treat each guest honorably.
He may be clearing you out
for some new delight.

The dark thought, the shame, the malice,
meet them at the door laughing,
and invite them in.

Be grateful for whoever comes,
because each has been sent
as a guide from beyond.

RUMI WAS A THIRTEENTH-CENTURY PERSIAN MUSLIM POET, JURIST, AND THEOLO-GIAN, BORN IN BALKH (PRESENT-DAY AFGHANISTAN). RUMI'S MAJOR WORK IS *MASNAVI-YE MANAVI* (SPIRITUAL COUPLETS), A SIX-VOLUME POEM REGARDED BY MANY SUFI MUSLIMS AS SECOND IN IMPORTANCE ONLY TO THE QUR'AN, ALONG WITH THE DIVAN-I KEBIR OR *DIWAN-E SHAMS-E TABRIZ-I* (THE WORKS OF SHAMS OF TABRIZ), COMPRISING SOME 40,000 VERSES.

I need this poem and read it often. The immediacy and abandon of Rumi's poetry helps me to know that the place which he inhabits is real, tangible and attainable. There is such sureness and security in his connection with the universe that more than any literature I've ever read, Rumi allows me to know that it is there and absolutely available to me and mankind...

-Alan Arkin

The Man Watching

RAINER MARIA RILKE
TRANSLATED BY ROBERT BLY

I can tell by the way the trees beat, after
so many dull days, on my worried windowpanes
that a storm is coming,
and I hear the far off fields say things
I can't bear without a friend,
I can't love without a sister.

The storm, the shifter of shapes, drives on
across the woods and across time,
and the world looks as if it had no age:
and landscape, like a line in the psalm book,
is seriousness and weight and eternity.

What we fight is so small!
What struggles with us is so great!
If only we would let ourselves be dominated
as things do by some immense storm,
we would become strong too, and not need names.

When we win it's with small things,
and the triumph itself makes us small.
What is extraordinary and eternal
does not want to be bent by us.
I mean the angel, who appeared
to the wrestler in the Old Testament:
When the wrestler's sinews
grew long like metal strings,
he felt them under his fingers
like chords of deep music.
Whoever was beaten by this Angel,
(who often simply declined the fight),
went away proud and strengthened
and great from that harsh hand,
that kneaded him as if to change his shape.

Winning does not tempt that one.
This is how he grows: by being defeated,
decisively, by constantly greater beings.

RAINER MARIA RILKE WAS BORN IN PRAGUE IN 1875. HIS FIRST GREAT WORK, *DAS STUNDEN BUCH* (*THE BOOK OF HOURS*), APPEARED IN 1906. WHEN WORLD WAR I BROKE OUT, RILKE LEFT FRANCE FOR MUNICH AND SPENT THE LAST YEARS OF HIS LIFE WRITING THE *DUINO ELEGIES* (1923) AND THE *SONNETS TO ORPHEUS* (1923). HE DIED OF LEUKEMIA IN 1926.

It's a peculiarly American stance that tells us winning is everything. In this frame of mind there's no room for worship, for adoration, for awe or even for significant growth. Rilke's poem knocks the pins right out of this position and he does it gracefully and with shocking dispatch, like a skillful Zen swordsman.

-Alan Arkin

JON ROBIN BAITZ

In Despair

CONSTANTINE CAVAFY
TRANSLATED BY DANIEL MENDELSOHN

He's lost him utterly. And from now on he seeks
in the lips of every new lover that he takes
the lips of that one: *his*. Coupling with every new
lover that he takes he longs to be mistaken:
that it's the same young man, that he's giving himself to *him*.

He's lost him utterly, as if he'd never been.
Because he wished—he said— he wished to save himself
from that stigmatized pleasure, so unwholesome;
from that stigmatized pleasure, in its shame.
There was still time, he said— time to save himself.

He's lost him utterly, as if he'd never been.
In his imagination, in his delusions
in the lips of other youths he seeks the lips of that one;
He wishes that he might feel his love again.

CONSTANTINE CAVAFY WAS BORN IN ALEXANDRIA, EGYPT, IN 1863. CAVAFY'S FAMILY MOVED TO ENGLAND IN 1870 AFTER HIS FATHER'S DEATH, WHERE HE BECAME SO COMFORTABLE WITH ENGLISH THAT HE WROTE HIS FIRST VERSE IN HIS SECOND LANGUAGE. CAVAFY NEVER OFFERED A VOLUME OF HIS POEMS FOR SALE, INSTEAD DISTRIBUTING PRIVATELY PRINTED PAMPHLETS TO FRIENDS AND RELATIVES. HE DIED IN 1933 FROM CANCER OF THE LARYNX.

The Cavafy poem entirely surrounds the pain and almost hallucinatory dislocation of romantic loss, and is filled with helpless youth, the kind that stays alive in us somewhere forever until the moment we die. It reminds me of pain forgotten, and the scar on my chest from open heart surgery. It makes me both smile at what we do to our poor selves—and wince at that very same thing.

-Jon Robin Baitz

Naming of Parts

HENRY REED

Today we have naming of parts. Yesterday,
We had daily cleaning. And tomorrow morning,
We shall have what to do after firing. But today,
Today we have naming of parts. Japonica
Glistens like coral in all of the neighboring gardens,
      And to-day we have naming of parts.

This is the lower sling swivel. And this
Is the upper sling swivel, whose use you will see,
When you are given your slings. And this is the piling swivel,
Which in your case you have not got. The branches
Hold in the gardens their silent, eloquent gestures,
      Which in our case we have not got.

This is the safety-catch, which is always released
With an easy flick of the thumb. And please do not let me
See anyone using his finger. You can do it quite easy
If you have any strength in your thumb. The blossoms
Are fragile and motionless, never letting anyone see
      Any of them using their finger.

And this you can see is the bolt. The purpose of this
Is to open the breech, as you see. We can slide it
Rapidly backwards and forwards: we call this
Easing the spring. And rapidly backwards and forwards
The early bees are assaulting and fumbling the flowers:
      They call it easing the Spring.

They call it easing the Spring: it is perfectly easy
If you have any strength in your thumb: like the bolt,
And the breech, and the cocking-piece, and the point of balance,
Which in our case we have not got; and the almond-blossom
Silent in all of the gardens and the bees going backwards and forwards,
      For today we have naming of parts.

HENRY REED WAS A WRITER AND TEACHER BORN IN ENGLAND IN 1914. HE WAS A FREELANCE JOURNALIST AND TEACHER IN BIRMINGHAM UNTIL BEING CALLED INTO SERVICE IN WWII. HIS ONLY BOOK OF POEMS, *A MAP OF VERONA*, WAS PUBLISHED IN 1946. REED WROTE MORE THAN FORTY RADIO PIECES FOR THE BBC BEFORE PASSING AWAY IN 1986.

NAMING OF PARTS more than any other poem seems written expressly for me and me alone. I possess it. I guard it. The exploration of duality, of simultaneous truths, contradiction and beauty; death and blood; florid scent and cold iron machinery of war, all a swirl in this tightly structured, even mechanical poem, which can barely contain the sum of its parts. I don't even know that it is a great poem, but hidden in its cool-headed and white-hot irony, I find a profoundly human riddle of being. So, for me, it is a truly magnificent piece of writing.

-Jon Robin Baitz

BOB
BALABAN

Paradox

CLARENCE R. WYLIE JR.

Not truth, nor certainty. These I forswore
In my novitiate, as young men called
To holy orders must abjure the world.
"If ..., then..." this only I assert;
And my successes are but pretty chains
Linking twin doubts, for it is vain to ask
If what I postulate be justified,
Or what I prove possess the stamp of fact.

Yet bridges stand, and men no longer crawl
In two dimensions. And such triumphs stem
In no small measure from the power this game,
Played with the thrice-attenuated shades
Of things, has over their originals.
How frail the wand, but how profound the spell!

CLARENCE R. WYLIE, JR. WAS A POET AND MATHEMATICS PROFESSOR AT FURMAN UNIVERSITY IN SOUTH CAROLINA. HE WROTE SEVERAL MATHEMATICS AND ENGINEERING TEXTBOOKS BEFORE HIS DEATH IN 1995 AT THE AGE OF 83.

We had to memorize this for tenth grade geometry class. The poem was supposed to make us understand the importance of plane geometry, make us work harder and do better in the subject. None of this happened. But the poem stuck. To me, it was a meditation on the arts and their relevance to the real and practical world around us. I think about this poem way too frequently.

—Bob Balaban

The Grasshopper and the Ant

JEAN DE LA FONTAINE
TRANSLATED BY ELIZUR WRIGHT

A Grasshopper gay
Sang the summer away,
And found herself poor
By the winter's first roar.
Of meat or of bread,
Not a morsel she had!
So a begging she went,
To her neighbour the ant,
    For the loan of some wheat,
    Which would serve her to eat,
Till the season came round.
    "I will pay you", she saith,
    "On an animal's faith,
Double weight in the pound
Ere the harvest be bound."
    The ant is a friend
    (And here she might mend)
    Little given to lend.
"How spent you the summer?"
    Quoth she, looking shame
    At the borrowing dame.
"Night and day to each comer
    I sang, if you please."
    "You sang! I'm at ease;
For 'tis plain at a glance,
Now, ma'am, you must dance."

Jean de la Fontaine, born in France in 1621, is best known for Fables, a collection of new and reworked fables. His most controversial series of poems, Contes, was deemed inappropriate and deferred his admission into the French Academy. He was elected into the Academy in 1684 after apologizing for his poetry's content and died in 1695.

I learned this poem in seventh grade French class and recite it to myself every few weeks because I love the way it sounds aloud. When I met Steven Spielberg for Close Encounters of the Third Kind, he asked me if I spoke French. As Francois Truffaut's interpreter in the movie, I would be required to do just that. I rattled off THE GRASSHOPPER AND THE ANT as "conversationally" as I could. No one in the room spoke French. They assumed I was fluent and I got the job.

-Bob Balaban

KEN
BRECHER

A Summer Night

W. H. AUDEN

Out on the lawn I lie in bed,
Vega conspicuous overhead
    In the windless nights of June,
As congregated leaves complete
Their day's activity; my feet
    Point to the rising moon.

Lucky, this point in time and space
Is chosen as my working-place,
    Where the sexy airs of summer,
The bathing hours and the bare arms,
The leisured drives through a land of farms,
    Are good to the newcomer.

Equal with colleagues in a ring
I sit on each calm evening,
    Enchanted as the flowers
The opening light draws out of hiding
From leaves with all its dove-like pleading
    Its logic and its powers;

That later we, though parted then,
May still recall these evenings when
    Fear gave his watch no look;
The lion griefs loped from the shade
And on our knees their muzzles laid,
    And Death put down his book.

Now north and south and east and west
Those I love lie down to rest;
    The moon look on them all,
The healers and the brilliant talkers,
The eccentrics and the silent walkers,
    The dumpy and the tall.

She climbs the European sky,
Churches and power-stations lie
    Alike among earth's fixtures:
Into the galleries she peers
And blankly as a butcher stares
    Upon the marvelous pictures.

To gravity attentive, she
Can notice nothing here, though we
    Whom hunger does not move,
From gardens where we feel secure
Look up and with a sigh endure
    The tyrannies of love:

And, gentle, do not care to know,
Where Poland draws her eastern bow,
    What violence is done,
Nor ask what doubtful act allows
Our freedom in this English house,
    Our picnics in the sun.

Soon, soon, through dykes of our content
The crumpling flood will force a rent
    And, taller than a tree,
Hold sudden death before our eyes
Whose river dreams long hid the size
    And vigours of the sea.

But when the waters make retreat
And through the black mud first the wheat
    In shy green stalks appears,
When stranded monsters gasping lie,
And sounds of riveting terrify
    Their whorled unsubtle ears,

May these delights we dread to lose,
This privacy, need no excuse
     But to that strength belong,
As through a child's rash happy rise
The drowned parental voices rise
     In unlamenting song.

After discharges of alarm
All unpredicted let them calm
     The pulse of nervous nations,
Forgive the murderer in his glass,
Tough in their patience to surpass
     The tigress her swift motions.

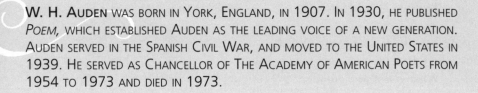

W. H. Auden was born in York, England, in 1907. In 1930, he published *Poem*, which established Auden as the leading voice of a new generation. Auden served in the Spanish Civil War, and moved to the United States in 1939. He served as Chancellor of The Academy of American Poets from 1954 to 1973 and died in 1973.

Four Quartets: East Coker (Section V)

T. S. ELIOT

So here I am, in the middle way, having had twenty years—
Twenty years largely wasted, the years of *l'entre deux guerres*.
Trying to learn to use words, and every attempt
Is a wholly new start, and a different kind of failure
Because one has only learnt to get the better of words
For the thing one no longer has to say, or the way in which
One is no longer disposed to say it. And so each venture
Is a new beginning, a raid on the inarticulate
With shabby equipment always deteriorating
In the general mess of imprecision of feeling,
Undisciplined squads of emotion. And what there is to conquer
By strength and submission, has already been discovered
Once or twice, or several times, by men whom one cannot hope
To emulate—but there is no competition—
There is only the fight to recover what has been lost
And found and lost again and again: and now, under conditions
That seem unpropitious. But perhaps neither gain nor loss.
For us, there is only the trying. The rest is not our business.

   Home is where one starts from. As we grow older
The world becomes stranger, the pattern more complicated
Of dead and living. Not the intense moment
Isolated, with no before and after,
But a lifetime burning in every moment
And not the lifetime of one man only
But of old stones that cannot be deciphered.
There is a time for the evening under starlight,
A time for the evening under lamplight
(The evening with the photograph album).
Love is most nearly itself
When here and now cease to matter.

Old men ought to be explorers
Here and there does not matter
We must be still and still moving
Into another intensity
For a further union, a deeper communion
Through the dark cold and the empty desolation,
The wave cry, the wind cry, the vast waters
Of the petrel and the porpoise.   In my end is my beginning.

T. S. ELIOT WAS BORN IN MISSOURI IN 1888. HIS FIRST BOOK OF POEMS, *PRUFROCK AND OTHER OBSERVATIONS,* IMMEDIATELY ESTABLISHED HIM AS A LEADING AVANT-GARDE POET. THE PUBLICATION OF *THE WASTE LAND* IN 1922 HELPED MAKE ELIOT A DOMINANT FIGURE IN POETRY AND LITERATURE. HE RECEIVED THE NOBEL PRIZE FOR LITERATURE IN 1948 AND DIED IN LONDON IN 1965.

I remember how puzzled I was when Sir William Hayter, the most distinguished man I had ever known, the head of my college at Oxford University, told me one summer evening in Italy that he could not remember ever feeling happier than he did at that moment. I was incredulous and thought that it could not possibly be true. From my twenty-something point of view, this great figure, an internationally respected diplomat at the end of a long and successful career, must have had happier moments. It was through poetry that I came to understand what Sir William must have felt that evening. It was all there, beautifully described, in W. H. Auden's poem A SUMMER NIGHT. I understood it when I read the fourth stanza. The evening in Italy is evoked so perfectly by Auden's imagery that in my mind's eye I can see the shooting stars and remember the smell of the air perfumed by ripening grapes. I feel certain that what made Sir William so happy is what now gives me much joy as well. He understood then what I feel now, for that brief moment death had most certainly put down his book.

It was another Oxford luminary, the anthropologist Rodney Needham, who gave me a gift of the Faber edition of T.S. Eliot's FOUR QUARTETS and told me to read EAST COKER and then come by for a chat. This was not an unusual request as he was my tutor when I was a graduate student studying for a degree in Social Anthropology. One afternoon each week, I would jump on my old black bicycle and pedal through the pouring rain to Dr. Needham's "rooms" in the Institute of Social Anthropology in north Oxford. I would sit in an uncomfortable wooden chair across from his desk and read aloud the two page essay I had been working on for the previous seven days.

The section of EAST COKER that Needham instructed me to read was number five (V). The poem became the subject of the first conversation we ever had that was not framed by our heretofore strictly teacher/student relationship. Needham had decided, he told me, that "we were to become friends" and that this change in our relationship should begin with my reading a particular section of Eliot's "Four Quartets." Needham was, at that time, in early middle age ("in the middle way") and I was shocked to discover that his books and essays which I greatly admired, in some cases revered, he dismissed with Eliot's words as nothing more than "a different kind of failure."

I felt honored to be let into this brilliant scholar's life, but although I read and reread the FOUR QUARTETS that had so clearly moved him, I was at a very different place in my life. I was in my early twenties, wanting to be in love, excited by what I was reading and learning and by what appealed to me in the academic life. I was a long way both physically and emotionally from the image of Eliot's "shabby equipment always deteriorating."

I never told Needham I could not connect to the poems he loved so much but he must have known it. What I think he wanted was to be sure that they would be there when I needed them and was ready to understand not only who he was but, perhaps, what I would one day be as well. He was right, bless him.

-Ken Brecher

STEVE
BUSCEMI

I Found a Dead Fox

MARY OLIVER

I found a dead fox
beside the gravel road,
curled inside the big
iron wheel

of an old tractor
that has been standing,
for years,
in the vines at the edge

of the road.
I don't know
what happened to it—
when it came there

or why it lay down
for good, settling
its narrow chin
on the rusted rim

of the iron wheel
to look out
over the fields,
and that way died—

but I know
this: its posture—
of looking,
to the last possible moment,

back into the world—
made me want
to sing something
joyous and tender

about foxes.
But what happened is this—
when I began,
when I crawled in

through the honeysuckle
and lay down,
curling my long spine
inside that cold wheel,

and touched the dead fox,
and looked out
into the wide fields,
the fox

vanished.
There was only myself
and the world,
and it was I

who was leaving.
And what could I sing
then?
Oh, beautiful world!

I just lay there
and looked at it.
And then it grew dark.
That day was done with.

And then the stars stepped forth
and held up their appointed
fires—
those hot, hard
watchmen of the night.

BRIAN COX

Ae fond kiss

ROBERT BURNS

Ae fond kiss, and then we sever;
Ae fareweel, alas, for ever!
Deep in heart-wrung tears I'll pledge thee,
Warring sighs and groans I'll wage thee!
Who shall say that Fortune grieves him
While the star of hope she leaves him?
Me, nae cheerfu' twinkle lights me,
Dark despair around benights me.

I'll ne'er blame my partial fancy;
Naething could resist my Nancy;
But to see her was to love her,
Love but her, and love for ever.
Had we never loved sae kindly,
Had we never loved sae blindly,
Never met—or never parted,
We had ne'er been broken-hearted.

Fare thee weel, thou first and fairest!
Fare thee weel, thou best and dearest!
Thine be ilka joy and treasure,
Peace, enjoyment, love, and pleasure.
Ae fond kiss, and then we sever;
Ae fareweel, alas, for ever!
Deep in heart-wrung tears I'll pledge thee,
Warring sighs and groans I'll wage thee.

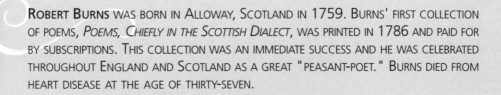

ROBERT BURNS WAS BORN IN ALLOWAY, SCOTLAND IN 1759. BURNS' FIRST COLLECTION OF POEMS, *POEMS, CHIEFLY IN THE SCOTTISH DIALECT*, WAS PRINTED IN 1786 AND PAID FOR BY SUBSCRIPTIONS. THIS COLLECTION WAS AN IMMEDIATE SUCCESS AND HE WAS CELEBRATED THROUGHOUT ENGLAND AND SCOTLAND AS A GREAT "PEASANT-POET." BURNS DIED FROM HEART DISEASE AT THE AGE OF THIRTY-SEVEN.

I Am

JOHN CLARE

I am—yet what I am none cares or knows,
My friends forsake me like a memory lost:—
I am the self-consumer of my woes:—
They rise and vanish in oblivion's host,
Like shadows in love's frenzied stifled throes:—
And yet I am, and live - like vapors tossed

Into the nothingness of scorn and noise,—
Into the living sea of waking dreams,
Where there is neither sense of life or joys,
But the vast shipwreck of my life's esteems;
Even the dearest, that I love the best,
Are strange - nay, rather stranger than the rest.

I long for scenes, where man has never trod;
A place where woman never smiled or wept;
There to abide with my creator, God;
And sleep as I in childhood sweetly slept:
Untroubling, and untroubled where I lie,
The grass below - above the vaulted sky.

JOHN CLARE, BORN IN HELPSTON, ENGLAND IN 1793, WAS COMMONLY KNOWN AS "THE NORTHAMPTONSHIRE PEASANT POET." HIS FIRST COLLECTION OF POEMS, *POEMS DESCRIPTIVE OF RURAL LIFE AND SCENERY*, WAS PUBLISHED IN 1820 TO MUCH ACCLAIM. CLARE SPENT THE LAST YEARS OF HIS LIFE IN AN ASYLUM, WHERE HE WROTE "I AM" AND DIED AT THE AGE OF SEVENTY-ONE.

These poems mean a great deal to me because both poets were ploughmen and of the land. They were both part of a major movement redefining poetry as no longer an expression of an academic poetic elite, but as an expression of the common man's political, aesthetic, and spiritual desires. Their work speaks to me because I feel it was a major reflection of the revolutionary fervour of the late 18th century and furthermore, I think both poems reflect the zeitgeist of unrest as demonstrated by the French and American revolutions.

-Brian Cox

PETER
COYOTE

Long-Legged Fly

W. B. YEATS

That civilization may not sink
Its great battle lost,
Quiet the dog, tether the pony
To a distant post.
Our master Caesar is in the tent
Where the maps are spread,
His eyes fixed upon nothing,
A hand under his head.

Like a long-legged fly upon the stream
His mind moves upon silence.

That the topless towers be burnt
And men recall that face,
Move most gently if move you must
In this lonely place.
She thinks, part woman, three parts a child,
That nobody looks; her feet
Practise a tinker shuffle
Picked up on the street.

Like a long-legged fly upon the stream
Her mind moves upon silence.

That girls at puberty may find
The first Adam in their thought,
Shut the door of the Pope's chapel,
Keep those children out.
There on the scaffolding reclines
Michael Angelo,
With no more sound than the mice make
His hand moves to and fro.

Like a long-legged fly upon the stream
His mind moves upon silence.

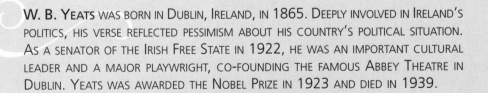

W. B. YEATS WAS BORN IN DUBLIN, IRELAND, IN 1865. DEEPLY INVOLVED IN IRELAND'S POLITICS, HIS VERSE REFLECTED PESSIMISM ABOUT HIS COUNTRY'S POLITICAL SITUATION. AS A SENATOR OF THE IRISH FREE STATE IN 1922, HE WAS AN IMPORTANT CULTURAL LEADER AND A MAJOR PLAYWRIGHT, CO-FOUNDING THE FAMOUS ABBEY THEATRE IN DUBLIN. YEATS WAS AWARDED THE NOBEL PRIZE IN 1923 AND DIED IN 1939.

This Tokyo

GARY SNYDER

Peace, war, religion
Revolution, will not help.
This horror seeds in the agile
Thumb and greedy little brain
That learned to catch bananas
With a stick.
  The millions of us worthless
To each other or the world
Or selves, the sufferers of the real
Or of the mind—this world
Is but a dream? Or human life
A nightmare grafted on solidity
Of planet—mental, mental
Shudder of the sun—praise
Evil submind freedom with de Sade
Or highest Dantean radiance of the God
Or endless Light or Life or Love
Or simple tinsel angel in the
Candy heaven of the poor—
Mental divinity or beauty, all,
Plato, Aquinas, Buddha,
Dionysius of the Cross, all
Pains or pleasures hells or
What in sense or flesh
Logic, eye, music, or
Concoction of all faculties
& thought tend—tend—to this:
  This gaudy apartment of the rich.

The comfort of the U.S. for its own.
The shivering pair of girls
Who dyked each other for a show
A thousand yen before us men
—In an icy room—to buy their relatives
A meal. This scramble spawn of
Wire dirt rails tin board blocks
Babies, students, crookt old men.
  We live
On the meeting of sun and earth.
We live—we live—and all our lives
Have led to this, this city,
Which is soon the world, this
Hopelessness where love of man
Or hate of man could matter
None, love if you will or
Contemplate or write or teach
But know in your human marrow you
Who read, that all you tread
Its earthquake rot and matter mental
Trembling, freedom is a void,
Peace war religion revolution
Will not help.

GARY SNYDER HAS PUBLISHED SIXTEEN BOOKS OF POETRY AND PROSE FOR WHICH HE HAS RECEIVED AN AMERICAN BOOK AWARD, A PULITZER PRIZE FOR POETRY AND PLACEMENT AS A FINALIST FOR THE NATIONAL BOOK AWARD. HE HAS RECEIVED AN AMERICAN ACADEMY OF ARTS AND LETTERS AWARD AND A GUGGENHEIM FOUNDATION FELLOWSHIP. HE IS A PROFESSOR OF ENGLISH AT THE UNIVERSITY OF CALIFORNIA, DAVIS.

This most Buddhist of Yeats' poems reminds me every time I read it of the absolute silence (read 'emptiness') on which the phenomenal world is based. The lightness of the LONG-LEGGED FLY moving with the flow is, somehow, the mind. The mind that makes war or peace is the mind that self-reflects and imitates and makes art. It is and is simultaneously 'of' the flow. I love this poem. Gary's poem is the perfect antidote to sentimental, romantic notions of progress and perfectability. This world of form is the world of greed, hatred, and delusion. Things which emerge as form, which are named, have beginnings and consequently endings, the path between is inevitable decay. Only the pure emptiness on which it is all based neither arrives or departs. There's nothing soft about this, nothing delusional, nothing comforting. It is Gary's diamond-hard insight cutting through Gordian knots of crap that make me value this poem so much.

-Peter Coyote

EVE ENSLER

i like my body when it is with you

E. E. CUMMINGS

i like my body when it is with your
body. It is so quite new a thing.
Muscles better and nerves more.
i like your body. i like what it does,
i like its hows. i like to feel the spine
of your body and its bones, and the trembling
-firm-smooth ness and which i will
again and again and again
kiss, i like kissing this and that of you,
i like,slowly stroking the,shocking fuzz
of your electric fur, and what-is-it comes
over parting flesh . . . . And eyes big love-crumbs,

and possibly i like the thrill

of under me you so quite new.

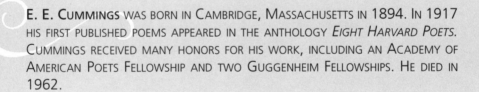

E. E. CUMMINGS WAS BORN IN CAMBRIDGE, MASSACHUSETTS IN 1894. IN 1917 HIS FIRST PUBLISHED POEMS APPEARED IN THE ANTHOLOGY *EIGHT HARVARD POETS*. CUMMINGS RECEIVED MANY HONORS FOR HIS WORK, INCLUDING AN ACADEMY OF AMERICAN POETS FELLOWSHIP AND TWO GUGGENHEIM FELLOWSHIPS. HE DIED IN 1962.

Epilogue

ANNA AKHMATOVA
TRANSLATED BY STANLEY KUNITZ

I

I have learned how faces fall to bone,
how under the eyelids terror lurks,
how suffering inscribes on cheeks
the hard lines of its cuneiform texts,
how glossy black or ash-fair locks
turn overnight to tarnished silver,
how smiles fade on submissive lips,
and fear quavers in a dry titter.
And I pray not for myself alone…
for all who stood outside the jail,
in bitter cold or summer's blaze,
with me under that blind red wall.

II

Remembrance hour returns with the turning year.
I see, I hear, I touch you drawing near:

the one we tried to help to the sentry's booth,
and who no longer walks this precious earth,

and that one who would toss her pretty mane
and say, "It's just like coming home again."

I want to name the names of all that host,
but they snatched up the list, and now it's lost.

I've woven them a garment that's prepared
out of poor words, those that I overheard,

and will hold fast to every word and glance
all of my days, even in new mischance,

and if a gag should blind my tortured mouth,
through which a hundred million people shout,

then let them pray for me, as I do pray
for them, this eve of my remembrance day.

And if my country ever should assent
to casting in my name a monument,

I should be proud to have my memory graced,
but only if the monument be placed

not near the sea on which my eyes first opened —
my last link with the sea has long been broken —

nor in the Tsar's garden near the sacred stump,
where a grieved shadow hunts my body's warmth,

but here, where I endured three hundred hours
in line before the implacable iron bars.

Because even in blissful death I fear
to lose the clangor of the Black Marias,

to lose the banging of that odious gate
and the old crone howling like a wounded beast.

And from my motionless bronze-lidded sockets
may the melting snow, like teardrops, slowly trickle,

and a prison dove coo somewhere, over and over,
as the ships sail softly down the flowing Neva.

ANNA AKHMATOVA WAS BORN IN ODESSA, UKRAINE, IN 1889. AHKMATOVA'S FIRST TWO PUBLICATIONS ESTABLISHED HER POSITIVE LITERARY REPUTATION, BUT THE POET'S WORK WAS BANNED FROM 1925 THROUGH 1940 DUE TO CONNECTIONS WITH HER EX-HUSBAND, AN OUTSPOKEN OPPONENT OF GOVERNMENTAL AFFAIRS. AHKMATOVA'S MOST ACCOMPLISHED WORKS, *REQUIEM* AND *POEM WITHOUT A HERO*, ARE REACTIONS TO THE HORROR OF THE STALINIST TERROR. AHKMATOVA DIED IN 1966.

Cummings's poem. So body. So poem becoming body. So words becoming flesh. Becoming touch, rhythms. I feel deep solace with Akhmatova's poem. There in the center of brutality, in the deepest injustice and imprisonment Anna "weaves a shroud with her words." Poetry does this. It documents and it imagines and it feels what is impossible and we go on.

-Eve Ensler

CARRIE FISHER

anyone lived in a little how town

E. E. CUMMINGS

anyone lived in a pretty how town
(with up so floating many bells down)
spring summer autumn winter
he sang his didn't he danced his did.

Women and men(both little and small)
cared for anyone not at all
they sowed their isn't they reaped their same
sun moon stars rain

children guessed(but only a few
and down they forgot as up they grew
autumn winter spring summer)
that noone loved him more by more

when by now and tree by leaf
she laughed his joy she cried his grief
bird by snow and stir by still
anyone's any was all to her

someones married their everyones
laughed their cryings and did their dance
(sleep wake hope and then)they
said their nevers they slept their dream

stars rain sun moon
(and only the snow can begin to explain
how children are apt to forget to remember
with up so floating many bells down)

one day anyone died i guess
(and noone stooped to kiss his face)
busy folk buried them side by side
little by little and was by was

all by all and deep by deep
and more by more they dream their sleep
noone and anyone earth by april
wish by spirit and if by yes.

Women and men(both dong and ding)
summer autumn winter spring
reaped their sowing and went their came
sun moon stars rain

E. E. Cummings WAS BORN IN CAMBRIDGE, MASSACHUSETTS IN 1894. IN 1917 HIS FIRST PUBLISHED POEMS APPEARED IN THE ANTHOLOGY *EIGHT HARVARD POETS.* CUMMINGS RECEIVED MANY HONORS FOR HIS WORK, INCLUDING AN ACADEMY OF AMERICAN POETS FELLOWSHIP AND TWO GUGGENHEIM FELLOWSHIPS. HE DIED IN 1962.

I love the language of this poem—he uses language in an incredibly unique way. He writes the sentences almost backwards but you hear the meaning as though forward. "Up so floating many bells down" may be one of my favorite sentences. It's so visual and lyrical.

-Carrie Fisher

This Be The Verse

PHILIP LARKIN

They fuck you up, your mum and dad,
They may not mean to, but they do.
They fill you with the faults they had,
And add some extra, just for you.

But they were fucked up in their turn,
By fools in old-style hats and coats,
Who half the time were soppy-stern,
And half at one another's throats.

Man hands on misery to man,
It deepens like a coastal shelf.
Get out as early as you can,
And don't have any kids yourself.

PHILIP LARKIN WAS BORN IN 1922 IN COVENTRY, ENGLAND. HIS FIRST BOOK OF POETRY, *THE NORTH SHIP*, WAS PUBLISHED IN 1945. LARKIN'S LATER COLLECTIONS, *THE LESS DECEIVED* AND THE WHITSUN WEDDINGS, ESTABLISHED HIS REPUTATION AS A MAJOR POET. LARKIN NEVER MARRIED AND WORKED AS A LIBRARIAN UNTIL HIS DEATH IN 1985.

Salman Rushdie told me why I like this poem—it's written in the style of children's verse, but with a very cynical, very adult message. And I always believe everything Salman says.
                                        -Carrie Fisher

MICHAEL
FITZGERALD

Four Quartets: East Coker

T. S. ELIOT

I
In my beginning is my end. In succession
Houses rise and fall, crumble, are extended,
Are removed, destroyed, restored, or in their place
Is an open field, or a factory, or a by-pass.
Old stone to new building, old timber to new fires,
Old fires to ashes, and ashes to the earth
Which is already flesh, fur and faeces,
Bone of man and beast, cornstalk and leaf.
Houses live and die: there is a time for building
And a time for living and for generation
And a time for the wind to break the loosened pane
And to shake the wainscot where the field-mouse trots
And to shake the tattered arras woven with a silent motto.

In my beginning is my end. Now the light falls
Across the open field, leaving the deep lane
Shuttered with branches, dark in the afternoon,
Where you lean against a bank while a van passes,
And the deep lane insists on the direction
Into the village, in the electric heat
Hypnotised. In a warm haze the sultry light
Is absorbed, not refracted, by grey stone.
The dahlias sleep in the empty silence.
Wait for the early owl.
                      In that open field
If you do not come too close, if you do not come too close,
On a summer midnight, you can hear the music
Of the weak pipe and the little drum
And see them dancing around the bonfire
The association of man and woman
In daunsinge, signifying matrimonie—
A dignified and commodious sacrament.
Two and two, necessarye coniunction,
Holding eche other by the hand or arm

Whiche betokeneth concorde. Round and round the fire
Leaping through the flames, or joined in circles,
Rustically solemn or in rustic laughter
Lifting heavy feet in clumsy shoes,
Earth feet, loam feet, lifted in country mirth
Mirth of those long since under earth
Nourishing the corn. Keeping time,
Keeping the rhythm in their dancing
As in their living in the living seasons
The time of the seasons and the constellations
The time of milking and the time of harvest
The time of the coupling of man and woman
And that of beasts. Feet rising and falling.
Eating and drinking. Dung and death.

Dawn points, and another day
Prepares for heat and silence. Out at sea the dawn wind
Wrinkles and slides. I am here
Or there, or elsewhere. In my beginning.

T. S. Eliot was born in Missouri in 1888. His first book of poems, *Prufrock and Other Observations,* immediately established him as a leading avant-garde poet. The publication of *The Waste Land* in 1922 helped make Eliot a dominant figure in poetry and literature. He received the Nobel Prize for Literature in 1948 and died in London in 1965.

"In my beginning is my end" and "In my end is my beginning" . . . . I am never quite sure where I've been after reading this or any of Eliot's other three Quartets but I am always in a state of heightened agitation and always completely at peace. Eliot is the only poet I know who can get away with writing "The poetry does not matter" with utter serenity when he means you to understand the exact opposite.

-Michael Fitzgerald

JANE
FONDA

from The Sonnets to Orpheus

RAINER MARIA RILKE
TRANSLATED BY DAVID YOUNG

Oh, this is the animal that never was.
They hadn't seen one; but just the same, they loved
its graceful movements, and the way it stood
looking at them calmly, with clear eyes.

It had not been. But for them, it appeared
in all its purity. They left space enough.
And in the space hollowed out by their love
it stood up all at once and didn't need

existence. They nourished it, not with grain,
but with the mere possibility of being.
And finally this gave so much power

that from its forehead a horn grew. One horn.
It drew near to a virgin, white, gleaming—
and was, inside the mirror and in her.

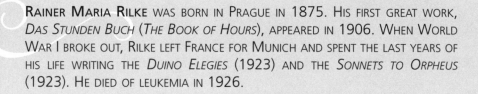

RAINER MARIA RILKE WAS BORN IN PRAGUE IN 1875. HIS FIRST GREAT WORK, *DAS STUNDEN BUCH* (*THE BOOK OF HOURS*), APPEARED IN 1906. WHEN WORLD WAR I BROKE OUT, RILKE LEFT FRANCE FOR MUNICH AND SPENT THE LAST YEARS OF HIS LIFE WRITING THE *DUINO ELEGIES* (1923) AND THE *SONNETS TO ORPHEUS* (1923). HE DIED OF LEUKEMIA IN 1926.

Moving Forward

RAINER MARIA RILKE
TRANSLATED BY ROBERT BLY

The deep parts of my life pour onward,
as if the river shores were opening out.
It seems that things are more like me now,
that I can see farther into paintings.
I feel closer to what language can't reach.
With my senses, as with birds, I climb
into the windy heaven, out of the oak,
and in the ponds broken off from the sky
my feeling sinks, as if standing on fishes.

ROBERT BLY IS A POET, TRANSLATOR, AND EDITOR. HE HAS AUTHORED MORE THAN TEN BOOKS OF TRANSLATIONS, INCLUDING *SELECTED POEMS OF RAINER MARIA RILKE*, AND MORE THAN THIRTY BOOKS OF POEMS, HIS MOST RECENT BEING *MY SENTENCE WAS A THOUSAND YEARS OF JOY: POEMS* (2006). HE CURRENTLY LIVES IN MINNESOTA WITH HIS FAMILY.

RODRIGO
GARCIA

Lament for Ignacio Sanchez Mejias

FEDERICO GARCIA LORCA
TRANSLATED BY STEPHEN SPENDER AND J.L. GILI

1. Cogida and Death

At five in the afternoon.
It was exactly five in the afternoon.
A boy brought the white sheet
at five in the afternoon.
A frail of lime ready prepared
at five in the afternoon.
The rest was death, and death alone
at five in the afternoon.

The wind carried away the cottonwool
at five in the afternoon.
And the oxide scattered crystal and nickel
at five in the afternoon.
Now the dove and the leopard wrestle
at five in the afternoon.
And a thigh with a desolated horn
at five in the afternoon.
The bass-string struck up
at five in the afternoon.
Arsenic bells and smoke
at five in the afternoon.
Groups of silence in the corners
at five in the afternoon.
And the bull alone with a high heart!
at five in the afternoon.
When the sweat of snow was coming
at five in the afternoon.
when the bull ring was covered with iodine
at five in the afternoon.
death laid eggs in the wound
at five in the afternoon.
At five in the afternoon.
Exactly at five o'clock in the afternoon.

A coffin on wheels is his bed
at five in the afternoon.
Bones and flutes resound in his ears
at five in the afternoon.
Now the bull was bellowing through his forehead
at five in the afternoon.
The room was iridiscent with agony
at five in the afternoon.
In the distance the gangrene now comes
at five in the afternoon.
Horn of the lily through green groins
at five in the afternoon.
The wounds were burning like suns
at five in the afternoon.

At five in the afternoon.
Ah, that fatal five in the afternoon!
It was five by all the clocks!
It was five in the shade of the afternoon!

2. The Spilled Blood

I will not see it!

Tell the moon to come,
for I do not want to see the blood
of Ignacio on the sand.

I will not see it!

The moon wide open.
Horse of still clouds,
and the grey bull ring of dreams
with willows in the barreras.

I will not see it!

Let my memory kindle!
Warm the jasmines
of such minute whiteness!

I will not see it!

The cow of the ancient world
passed her sad tongue
over a snout of blood
spilled on the sand,
and the bulls of Guisando,
partly death and partly stone,
bellowed like two centuries
sated with threading the earth.
No.
I do not want to see it!
I will not see it!
Ignacio goes up the tiers
with all his death on his shoulders.
He sought for the dawn
but the dawn was no more.
He seeks for his confident profile
and the dream bewilders him.
He sought for his beautiful body
and encountered his opened blood.
I will not see it!
I do not want to hear it spurt
each time with less strength:
that spurt that illuminates
the tiers of seats, and spills
over the cordury and the leather
of a thirsty multiude.
Who shouts that I should come near!
Do not ask me to see it!

His eyes did not close
when he saw the horns near,
but the terrible mothers
lifted their heads.

And across the ranches,
an air of secret voices rose,
shouting to celestial bulls,
herdsmen of pale mist.
There was no prince in Seville
who could compare to him,
nor sword like his sword
nor heart so true.
Like a river of lions
was his marvellous strength,
and like a marble toroso
his firm drawn moderation.
The air of Andalusian Rome
gilded his head
where his smile was a spikenard
of wit and intelligence.
What a great torero in the ring!
What a good peasant in the sierra!
How gentle with the sheaves!
How hard with the spurs!
How tender with the dew!
How dazzling in the fiesta!
How tremendous with the final
banderillas of darkness!

But now he sleeps without end.
Now the moss and the grass
open with sure fingers
the flower of his skull.
And now his blood comes out singing;
singing along marshes and meadows,
sliding on frozen horns,
faltering soulless in the mist
stumbling over a thousand hoofs
like a long, dark, sad tongue,
to form a pool of agony
close to the starry Guadalquivir.
Oh, white wall of Spain!

Oh, black bull of sorrow!
Oh, hard blood of Ignacio!
Oh, nightingale of his veins!
No.
I will not see it!
No chalice can contain it,
no swallows can drink it,
no frost of light can cool it,
nor song nor deluge of white lilies,
no glass can cover it with silver.
No.
I will not see it!

FEDERICO GARCIA LORCA WAS BORN NEAR GRANADA IN 1899. HE WROTE SEVERAL PLAYS AND POETRY BOOKS, INCLUDING *ROMANCERO GITANO* (THE GYPSY BALLADS), WHICH HAS BEEN REPRINTED SEVERAL TIMES. WHILE STAYING IN MADRID IN 1936, GARCIA LORCA WAS SHOT TO DEATH AND LEFT IN AN UNIDENTIFIED GRAVE BY CIVIL WAR SOLDIERS; HIS BURIAL LOCATION REMAINS UNKNOWN.

Ode to the Artichoke

PABLO NERUDA
TRANSLATED BY JODEY BATEMAN

The artichoke
With a tender heart
Dressed up like a warrior,
Standing at attention, it built
A small helmet
Under its scales
It remained
Unshakeable,
By its side
The crazy vegetables
Uncurled
Their tendrills and leaf-crowns,
Throbbing bulbs,
In the sub-soil
The carrot
With its red mustaches
Was sleeping,
The grapevine
Hung out to dry its branches
Through which the wine will rise,
The cabbage
Dedicated itself
To trying on skirts,
The oregano
To perfuming the world,
And the sweet
Artichoke
There in the garden,
Dressed like a warrior,
Burnished
Like a proud
Pomegrante.

And one day
Side by side
In big wicker baskets
Walking through the market
To realize their dream
The artichoke army
In formation.
Never was it so military
Like on parade.
The men
In their white shirts
Among the vegetables
Were
The Marshals
Of the artichokes
Lines in close order
Command voices, take over
And the bang
Of a falling box.

But
Then
Maria
Comes
With her basket.
She chooses
An artichoke,
She's not afraid of it.
She examines it, she observes it
Up against the light like it was an egg, She buys it, She mixes it up
In her handbag
With a pair of shoes
With a cabbage head and a
Bottle
Of vinegar
Until
She enters the kitchen
And submerges it in a pot.

Thus ends
In peace
This career
Of the armed vegetable
Which is called an artichoke,
Then
Scale by scale,
We strip off
The delicacy
And eat
The peaceful mush
Of its green heart.

PABLO NERUDA WAS BORN IN SOUTHERN CHILE IN 1904. IN 1923, HE SOLD ALL OF HIS POSSESSIONS TO FINANCE THE PUBLICATION OF HIS FIRST BOOK, *CREPUSCULARIO* (TWILIGHT). NERUDA RECEIVED NUMEROUS AWARDS, INCLUDING THE INTERNATIONAL PEACE PRIZE, THE LENIN PEACE PRIZE, THE STALIN PEACE PRIZE, AND THE NOBEL PRIZE FOR LITERATURE. HE DIED OF LEUKEMIA IN 1973.

These two poems I read at about the same time in my very early teens, one playful and the other tragic. Both are accessible and powerful and made me a life-long fan of poetry and of what poetry can do—and taught me how all other art forms aspire to poetry, to the things that can only be said with the tools of poetry.
-Rodrigo Garcia

KATHLEEN GLYNN

TRACKS 4,5

My Son, My Executioner

DONALD HALL

My son, my executioner,
   I take you in my arms,
Quiet and small and just astir
And whom my body warms.

Sweet death, small son, our instrument
   Of immortality,
Your cries and hunger document
Our bodily decay.

We twenty-five and twenty-two
   Who seemed to live forever
Observe enduring life in you
And start to die together.

DONALD HALL WAS BORN IN NEW HAVEN, CONNECTICUT, IN 1928. HE HAS PUBLISHED NUMEROUS POETRY COLLECTIONS INCLUDING *THE ONE DAY* (1988), WHICH WON THE NATIONAL BOOK CRITICS CIRCLE AWARD, THE *LOS ANGELES TIMES* BOOK PRIZE, AND A PULITZER PRIZE NOMINATION. HALL SERVED AS POET LAUREATE OF NEW HAMPSHIRE FROM 1984 TO 1989, AND AS POET LAUREATE OF THE UNITED STATES FOR 2007.

The Shipfitter's Wife

DORIANNE LAUX

I loved him most
when he came home from work,
his fingers still curled from fitting pipe,
his denim shirt ringed with sweat
and smelling of salt, the drying weeds
of the ocean. I'd go to where he sat
on the edge of the bed, his forehead
anointed with grease, his cracked hands
jammed between his thighs, and unlace
the steel-toed boots, stroke his ankles,
his calves, the pads and bones of his feet.
Then I'd open his clothes and take
the whole day inside me—the ship's
gray sides, the miles of copper pipe,
the voice of the foreman clanging
off the hull's silver ribs. Spark of lead
kissing metal. The clamp, the winch,
the white fire of the torch, the whistle
and the long drive home.

DORIANNE LAUX IS THE AUTHOR OF *WHAT WE CARRY* (1994), FINALIST FOR THE NATIONAL BOOK CRITICS CIRCLE AWARD, AND *AWAKE* (1990), NOMINATED FOR THE SAN FRANCISCO BAY AREA BOOK CRITICS AWARD FOR POETRY. LAUX IS AN ASSOCIATE PROFESSOR AT THE UNIVERSITY OF OREGON'S PROGRAM IN CREATIVE WRITING, AND SHE LIVES IN EUGENE, OREGON, WITH HER HUSBAND, POET JOSEPH MILLAR.

I went to hear Donald Hall read in the Ann Arbor area when I was about 24. The poem and the night never left me—made quite an impression. I can always recite it (and others). He's a bit of a rock god to me.

-Kathleen Glynn

PAUL GUILFOYLE

TRACKS 6,7

Casualty

SEAMUS HEANEY

I
He would drink by himself
And raise a weathered thumb
Towards the high shelf,
Calling another rum
And blackcurrant, without
Having to raise his voice,
Or order a quick stout
By a lifting of the eyes
And a discreet dumb-show
Of pulling off the top;
At closing time would go
In waders and peaked cap
Into the showery dark,
A dole-kept breadwinner
But a natural for work.
I loved his whole manner,
Sure-footed but too sly,
His deadpan sidling tact,
His fisherman's quick eye
And turned observant back.

Incomprehensible
To him, my other life.
Sometimes, on the high stool,
Too busy with his knife
At a tobacco plug
And not meeting my eye,
In the pause after a slug
He mentioned poetry.

We would be on our own
And, always politic
And shy of condescension,
I would manage by some trick
To switch the talk to eels
Or lore of the horse and cart
Or the Provisionals.

But my tentative art
His turned back watches too:
He was blown to bits
Out drinking in a curfew
Others obeyed, three nights
After they shot dead
The thirteen men in Derry.
PARAS THIRTEEN, the walls said,
BOGSIDE NIL. That Wednesday
Everyone held
His breath and trembled.

II
It was a day of cold
Raw silence, wind-blown
Surplice and soutane:
Rained-on, flower-laden
Coffin after coffin
Seemed to float from the door
Of the packed cathedral
Like blossoms on slow water.
The common funeral
Unrolled its swaddling band,
Lapping, tightening
Till we were braced and bound
Like brothers in a ring.

But he would not be held
At home by his own crowd
Whatever threats were phoned,
Whatever black flags waved.
I see him as he turned
In that bombed offending place,
Remorse fused with terror
In his still knowable face,
His cornered outfaced stare
Blinding in the flash.

He had gone miles away
For he drank like a fish
Nightly, naturally
Swimming towards the lure
Of warm lit-up places,
The blurred mesh and murmur
Drifting among glasses
In the gregarious smoke.
How culpable was he
That last night when he broke
Our tribe's complicity?
'Now, you're supposed to be
An educated man,'
I hear him say. 'Puzzle me
The right answer to that one.'

III
I missed his funeral,
Those quiet walkers
And sideways talkers
Shoaling out of his lane
To the respectable
Purring of the hearse...
They move in equal pace
With the habitual
Slow consolation
Of a dawdling engine,
The line lifted, hand
Over fist, cold sunshine
On the water, the land
Banked under fog: that morning
I was taken in his boat,
The screw purling, turning
Indolent fathoms white,
I tasted freedom with him.
To get out early, haul
Steadily off the bottom,
Dispraise the catch, and smile
As you find a rhythm
Working you, slow mile by mile,
Into your proper haunt
Somewhere, well out, beyond...

Dawn-sniffing revenant,
Plodder through midnight rain,
Question me again.

SEAMUS HEANEY WAS BORN IN 1939 IN NORTHERN IRELAND. HE HAS PUBLISHED SEVERAL POETRY COLLECTIONS INCLUDING *OPENED GROUND* (1999). IN 1995, HE RECEIVED THE NOBEL PRIZE IN LITERATURE. HEANEY IS A DUBLIN RESIDENT, BUT SINCE 1981 HE HAS SPENT PART OF EACH YEAR TEACHING AT HARVARD UNIVERSITY, WHERE IN 1984 HE WAS ELECTED THE BOYLSTON PROFESSOR OF RHETORIC AND ORATORY.

To His Coy Mistress

ANDREW MARVELL

Had we but world enough, and time,
This coyness, lady, were no crime.
We would sit down, and think which way
To walk, and pass our long love's day.
Thou by the Indian Ganges' side
Shouldst rubies find; I by the tide
Of Humber would complain. I would
Love you ten years before the Flood;
And you should, if you please, refuse
Till the conversion of the Jews.
My vegetable love should grow
Vaster than empires, and more slow.
An hundred years should go to praise
Thine eyes, and on thy forehead gaze.
Two hundred to adore each breast:
But thirty thousand to the rest.
An age at least to every part,
And the last age should show your heart:
For, Lady, you deserve this state;
Nor would I love at lower rate.
    But at my back I always hear
Time's winged chariot hurrying near:
And yonder all before us lie
Deserts of vast eternity.
Thy beauty shall no more be found;
Nor, in thy marble vault, shall sound
My echoing song: then worms shall try
That long-preserv'd virginity,
And your quaint honour turn to dust;
And into ashes all my lust.
The grave's a fine and private place,
But none, I think, do there embrace.

Now, therefore, while the youthful hue
Sits on thy skin like morning dew,
And while thy willing soul transpires
At every pore with instant fires,
Now let us sport us while we may;
And now, like amorous birds of prey,
Rather at once our time devour,
Than languish in his slow-chapped power.
Let us roll all our strength, and all
Our sweetness, up into one ball:
And tear our pleasures with rough strife
Thorough the iron gates of life.
Thus, though we cannot make our sun
Stand still, yet we will make him run.

ANDREW MARVELL, BORN IN 1621, GREW UP IN THE YORKSHIRE TOWN OF HULL. MARVELL'S POLITICAL CONNECTION AS PARLIAMENT MEMBER KEPT HIM FROM PUBLISHING MANY OF HIS POEMS DURING HIS LIFETIME, MOST FOCUSING ON HIS CRITICISMS OF THE GOVERNMENT FOR WHICH HE WORKED. A COLLECTION OF MARVELL'S WORK, COMPILED BY HIS NEPHEW, DID NOT APPEAR UNTIL THREE YEARS AFTER HIS DEATH IN 1678.

Seamus Heaney galvanized an experience that I felt growing up in South Boston, a strong Irish Catholic working environment, when it was transitioning into something other than immigrant struggle after Korean War. It's now a kind of proud working class without the armor or patina of work. There is a pride in the class, not pride in their work. This poem reminds me of when I was a little boy in the 1950s. It was different. Starting as a child I remember: there was WORK and Mass and work and camel untipped cigarettes and work and parades and soda bread and work and scully caps and beer and whiskey and work and callused hands and music and boxing and a coughing kind of laughter and yelling and blood and work and no loose change, all money either saved or spent. The feelings that poem evoked (and I went to readings of Heaney's later in Boston), gave me the anvil that my hammer could land on, helped me understand and allowed me to recognize the struggle of my working background; the cupcake without the frosting that everyone was trying to ladle on to sweeten the pain, that frosting of catholic parochial mendacity came off with this poem's message. Heaney's poem was about Ireland, but it sure felt like the docks where my uncles and even I worked for a time in South Boston. It was also about a character which I found easy to use eyes to see. That's why I like acting, I guess. This was truth with the simultaneous relief of pain that comes with knowing and it informs my work to this day. It also cemented a respect for anyone who works at anything. And in the classic sense: As a schoolboy, I used to recite Marvell's TO HIS COY MISTRESS to girls in the hope of getting laid, but found out all the educated boys of my world (and there were many baby boomer youth) were doing the same, and I fell into cliché.

Mary Oliver and Stanley Kunitz, Gregory Corso, Robert Bly... I appreciated their poems as authentic stamps of their experience. Not necessarily mine, but I felt the truth in them. Acting, on one level, is a revelation of a process in motion, as water, done in public view, an unravelling or ravelling. Poetry for me is the result of that ravelling done in private and then the essence is sculpted into a form. Mary Oliver's *When Death Comes* is an example of this personal authenticity. There are poets who I admire for the craft and intensity of their work. W.B. Yeats, Ted Hughes, Catullus, Walt Whitman, Ovid, E. E. Cummings, Ginsberg. Dylan Thomas. I think of Eugene O'Neill, Lou Reed, Bob Dylan, Joni Mitchell, and Wu-Tang Clan as poets, as well, but because I saw them in a performance it's more like theatre. Also, any sections of Virgil's *Aeneid*, the travels especially with Charon the boatman, the Dido relationship, and any part of the large epic poem that expresses the need to journey, the courage to face the unknown, alone. Homer's *Iliad* and *Odyssey* are similar. I worked on these poems in Latin and Greek for six years. I worked on and published a translation of Horace's *An Ode To Phyrrus*.

So...that's my confession.

-Paul Guilfoyle

DARYL
HANNAH

On the Great Joy of the Stars

BLAISE CENDRARS

On the axis of Noon, the mouth of the grotto opens and startles you like a blue buttercup: inside, the meticulous progress of the planets can be watched. Nothing is as simple, grand, calm, and serene as this sight, nothing else releases so much happiness. A phonograph record that turns, but without anything mechanical. Chinese music. Up in Tibet, the sturdy gong of contemplation. In some rock crystals you see the ring of Venus like the neck of a black giraffe, speckled Jupiter, the jungle of Mars, Earth, inalterable as platinum. In these meadows, breathing is a wild horse.

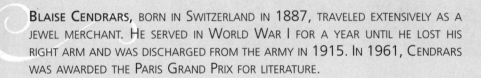

BLAISE CENDRARS, BORN IN SWITZERLAND IN 1887, TRAVELED EXTENSIVELY AS A JEWEL MERCHANT. HE SERVED IN WORLD WAR I FOR A YEAR UNTIL HE LOST HIS RIGHT ARM AND WAS DISCHARGED FROM THE ARMY IN 1915. IN 1961, CENDRARS WAS AWARDED THE PARIS GRAND PRIX FOR LITERATURE.

I have Blaise Cendrars's poem ON THE GREAT JOY OF STARS written on the wall in the outhouse at the old stagecoach stop where I live in the mountains... might seem like a strange place but it can be a good place to ponder things. This poem takes my breath away every time I read it...so unexpected in its combination of images yet somehow so perfect it speaks to me of the interconnectedness of things, it makes my brain expand and feel like I can breathe.

-Daryl Hannah

Ode to the Hummingbird

PABLO NERUDA
TRANSLATED BY MARIA JACKETTI

Flying spark of water.
Incandescent drop of American fire.
Lighted summary of jungle,
Precise celestial rainbow:
To the hummingbird a bow,
A thread of gold.
A flame of green!

Oh minimum living flash of lightning,
When unmoving in air your structure
Of pollen, feather or burning ember.
I ask, what are you?
Where did you originate?

Perhaps it was during the Flood.
In the fertile primordial mud.
When the rose in anthracite was congealed,
And metallic elements annealed,
Each in its secret gallery.

'Twas then from a wounded saurian
rolled a fragment.
An atom of gold,
The last cosmic scale,
A drop of earthen fire flew
Suspending your beauty,
You iridescent and quick sapphire.

You sleep in a nut,
Fit in a miniscule corolla
An arrow true, shield,
Honeyed vibration, ray of pollen,
You're so brave, the feathered armor

Of the black falcon won't scare you:
You gyrate like light within light,
Air in air,
Intrepidly you venture
Into the humid sheath of a tremulous flower,
Fearless that its nuptial honey will decapitate you.

From scarlet to powdered gold,
From burning yellow,
To the rare emerald green,
In velvet orange and black
Your scintillant corset
From a pointed amber thorn you begin,
Tiny supreme being,
A miracle you are, and burn from
California's heat
To whistling windy Patagonia

Seed of sun, feathered flame,
Miniscule flying flag,
Petals of silenced warriors,
Silable of the buried blood.
Crown of the submerged antique heart.

PABLO NERUDA WAS BORN IN SOUTHERN CHILE IN 1904. IN 1923, HE SOLD ALL OF HIS POSSESSIONS TO FINANCE THE PUBLICATION OF HIS FIRST BOOK, *CREPUSCULARIO* (TWILIGHT). NERUDA RECEIVED NUMEROUS AWARDS, INCLUDING THE INTERNATIONAL PEACE PRIZE, THE LENIN PEACE PRIZE, THE STALIN PEACE PRIZE, AND THE NOBEL PRIZE FOR LITERATURE. HE DIED OF LEUKEMIA IN 1973.

*It's the perfect, most poetic, flawless, evocative, in cadence and word,
description of a hummingbird I could ever imagine.*
-Daryl Hannah

PHILIP
SEYMOUR
HOFFMAN

Inventing a Horse

MEGHAN O'ROURKE

Inventing a horse is not easy.
One must not only think of the horse.
One must dig fence posts around him.
One must include a place where horses like to live;

or do when they live with humans like you.
Slowly, you must walk him in the cold;
feed him bran mash, apples;
accustom him to the harness;

holding in mind even when you are tired
harnesses and tack cloths and saddle oil
to keep the saddle clean as a face in the sun;
one must imagine teaching him to run

among the knuckles of tree roots,
not to be skittish at first sight of timber wolves,
and not to grow thin in the city,
where at some point you will have to live;

and one must imagine the absence of money.
Most of all though: the living weight,
the sound of his feet on the needles,
and, since he is heavy, and real,

and sometimes tired after a run
down the river with a light whip at his side,
one must imagine love
in the mind that does not know love,

an animal mind, a love that does not depend
on your image of it,
your understanding of it;
indifferent to all that it lacks:

a muzzle and two black eyes
looking the day away, a field empty
of everything but witch grass, fluent trees,
and some piles of hay.

MEGHAN O'ROURKE GREW UP IN BROOKLYN, NEW YORK, AND BEGAN HER LITERARY CAREER AT THE *NEW YORKER* IN 1997. IN 2007, HER FIRST BOOK OF POETRY, *HALFLIFE*, WAS PUBLISHED. HER POEMS HAVE APPEARED IN THE *NEW YORKER* AND, THE *NEW YORK REVIEW OF BOOKS*, AND HER PROSE IN THE *NEW YORK TIMES BOOK REVIEW* AND THE *LOS ANGELES TIMES BOOK REVIEW*.

The People Who Succeed…

EUGENE O'NEILL

The people who succeed and do not push on to a greater failure are the spiritual middle-classers.

Their stopping at success is the proof of their compromising insignificance. How petty their dreams must have been!

Those who pursue the mere attainable should be sentenced to get it—and keep it.

Let them rest on their laurels and enthrone them in Morris chairs in which laurels and hero may wither together.

Only through the unattainable do we achieve a hope worth both living and dying for—and so attain ourselves.

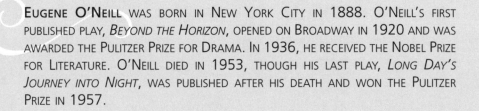

EUGENE O'NEILL WAS BORN IN NEW YORK CITY IN 1888. O'NEILL'S FIRST PUBLISHED PLAY, *BEYOND THE HORIZON*, OPENED ON BROADWAY IN 1920 AND WAS AWARDED THE PULITZER PRIZE FOR DRAMA. IN 1936, HE RECEIVED THE NOBEL PRIZE FOR LITERATURE. O'NEILL DIED IN 1953, THOUGH HIS LAST PLAY, *LONG DAY'S JOURNEY INTO NIGHT*, WAS PUBLISHED AFTER HIS DEATH AND WON THE PULITZER PRIZE IN 1957.

STACY KEACH

TRACKS 8,9

Sonnet 30

WILLIAM SHAKESPEARE

When to the sessions of sweet silent though
I summon up remembrance of things past,
I sigh the lack of many a thing I sought,
And with old woes new wail my dear time's waste;
Then can I drown an eye, unused to flow,
For precious friends hid in death's dateless night,
And weep afresh love's long since cancell'd woe,
And moan the expense of many a vanished sight.
Then can I grieve at grievances foregone,
And heavily from woe to woe tell o'er
The sad account of fore-bemoanéd moan,
Which I new pay as if not paid before.
    But if the while I think on thee, dear friend,
    All losses are restored and sorrows end.

WILLIAM SHAKESPEARE WAS BORN IN 1564 IN STRATFORD-ON-AVON. IN 1594, SHAKESPEARE JOINED THE LORD CHAMBERLAIN'S COMPANY OF ACTORS, THE MOST POPULAR COMPANY ACTING AT COURT. SHAKESPEARE'S SONNETS WERE COMPOSED BETWEEN 1593 AND 1601, THOUGH THEY WERE NOT PUBLISHED UNTIL 1609 AS *THE SONNETS OF SHAKESPEARE* CONSISTING OF 154 SONNETS. HE DIED IN 1616.

Shakespeare has always been a source of inspiration and sustenance for me, and this particular sonnet uniquely expresses a universal sentiment about what it means to be able to emerge from the inevitable human condition of grief and despair. The last line, "But if the while I think on thee, dear friend,/All losses are restored and sorrows end," for me embodies all that is necessary to rise above self-pity and sadness.

-Stacy Keach

The Invitation

ORIAH MOUNTAIN DREAMER

It doesn't interest me what you do for a living. I want to know what you ache for, and if you dare to dream of meeting your heart's longing.

It doesn't interest me how old you are. I want to know if you will risk looking like a fool for love, for your dreams, for the adventure of being alive.

It doesn't interest me what planets are squaring your moon. I want to know if you have touched the center of your own sorrow, if you have been opened by life's betrayals or have become shriveled and closed from fear of further pain. I want to know if you can sit with pain, mine or your own, without moving to hide it, or fade it, or fix it.

I want to know if you can be with joy, mine or your own, if you can dance with wildness and let the ecstasy fill you to the tips of your fingers and toes without cautioning us to be careful, to be realistic, to remember the limitations of being human.

It doesn't interest me if the story you are telling me is true. I want to know if you can disappoint another to be true to yourself; if you can bear the accusation of betrayal and not betray your own soul; if you can be faithless and therefore trustworthy.

I want to know if you can see beauty even when it's not pretty, every day, and if you can source your own life from its presence.

I want to know if you can live with failure, yours and mine, and still stand at the edge of the lake and shout to the silver of the full moon, "Yes!"

It doesn't interest me to know where you live or how much money you have. I want to know if you can get up, after the night of grief and despair, weary and bruised to the bone, and do what needs to be done to feed the children.

It doesn't interest me to know who you know or how you came to be here. I want to know if you will stand in the center of the fire with me and not shrink back.

It doesn't interest me where or what or with whom you have studied. I want to know what sustains you, from the inside, when all else falls away.

I want to know if you can be alone with yourself and if you truly like the company you keep in the empty moments.

ORIAH MOUNTAIN DREAMER IS A PUBLIC SPEAKER AND BESTSELLING AUTHOR OF INSPIRATIONAL PROSE BOOKS, *THE INVITATION*, *THE DANCE*, AND *THE CALL*. HER MOST RECENT WORK, *WHAT WE ACHE FOR*, WAS PUBLISHED IN 2005. ORIAH HAS ALSO LED MANY NATIONWIDE WORKSHOPS ON HOW TO LIVE A FULFILLED LIFE. SHE CURRENTLY LIVES IN CANADA WITH HER HUSBAND.

I have only recently come to know Oriah Mountain Dreamer's work, and this particular prose-poem arouses deep feelings of joy and love. It encourages me to live my life with a sharpened sense of honesty. It fills my heart and soul with the comforting notion that it is okay to dare to dream in spite of setbacks. Here, the last line rings with truth. "I want to know if you can be alone with yourself and if you truly like the company you keep in the empty moments."

-Stacy Keach

SWOOSIE
KURTZ

From A Norman Crucifix of 1632

CHARLES CAUSLEY

I am the great sun, but you do not see me,
　I am your husband, but you turn away,
I am the captive, but you do not free me,
　I am the captain you will not obey.

I am the truth, but you will not believe me,
　I am the city where you will not stay,
I am your wife, your child, but you will leave me,
　I am that God to whom you will not pray.

I am your counsel, but you do not hear me,
　I am the lover whom you will betray,
I am the victor, but you do not cheer me,
　I am the holy dove whom you will slay.

I am your life, but if you will not name me,
Seal up your soul with tears, and never blame me.

CHARLES CAUSLEY WAS BORN IN CORNWALL, ENGLAND IN 1917. AFTER SERVING IN THE NAVY DURING WORLD WAR II, CAUSLEY REGULARLY PUBLISHED SHORT STORY AND POETRY COLLECTIONS, STARTING WITH *HANDS TO DANCE* AND *FAREWELL, AGGIE WESTON* IN 1951. HE RECEIVED MANY HONORS FOR HIS WORK, INCLUDING BECOMING A FELLOW OF THE ROYAL SOCIETY OF LITERATURE IN 1958. CAUSLEY PASSED AWAY IN 2003.

Death of a Son

JON SILKIN

Something has ceased to come along with me.
Something like a person: something very like one.
And there is no nobility in it
Or anything like that.

Something was there like a one year
Old house, dumb as stone. While the near buildings
Sang like birds and laughed
Understanding the pact

They were to have with silence. But he
Neither sang nor laughed. He did not bless silence
Like bread, with words.
He did not forsake silence.

But rather, like a house in mourning
Kept the eye turned in to watch the silence while
The other houses like birds
Sang around him.

And the breathing silence neither
Moved nor was still.
I have seen stones: I have seen brick
But this house was made up of neither bricks nor stone
But a house of flesh and blood
With flesh of stone

And bricks for blood. A house
Of stones and blood in breathing silence with the other
Birds singing crazy on its chimneys.
But this was silence,

This was something else, this was
Hearing and speaking though he was a house drawn
Into silence, this was
Something religious in his silence,

Something shining in his quiet,
This was different, this was altogether something else:
Though he never spoke, this
Was something to do with death.

And then slowly the eye stopped looking
Inward. The silence rose and became still.
The look turned to the outer place and stopped,
With the birds still shrilling around him.
And as if he could speak

He turned over on his side with his one year
Red as a wound
He turned over as if he could be sorry for this
And out of his eyes two great tears rolled, like stones,
and he died.

JON SILKIN, BORN IN LONDON IN 1930, WAS AN ACCLAIMED POET WHOSE FIRST COLLECTION OF POETRY, *THE PEACEABLE KINGDOM*, WAS PUBLISHED IN 1954. ASIDE FROM HIS NUMEROUS WORKS OF POETRY, SILKIN WAS A GREGORY FELLOW IN POETRY AT THE UNIVERSITY OF LEEDS FOR TWO YEARS AS WELL AS FOUNDER AND EDITOR OF THE POETRY MAGAZINE, *STAND*, FROM 1952 UNTIL HIS DEATH IN 1997.

I relate so strongly to FROM A NORMAN CRUCIFIX because I feel the poet is speaking directly to me about my life. Then about the Silkin—it is so deeply moving & disturbing, even more so because the poet understates everything so matter-of-factly.

-Swoosie Kurtz

MICHAEL LALLY

TRACKS 10,11

Danse Russe

WILLIAM CARLOS WILLIAMS

If I when my wife is sleeping
and the baby and Kathleen
are sleeping
and the sun is a flame-white disc
in silken mists
above shining trees,—
if I in my north room
dance naked, grotesquely
before my mirror
waving my shirt round my head
and singing softly to myself:
"I am lonely, lonely,
I was born to be lonely,
I am best so!"
If I admire my arms, my face,
my shoulders, flanks, buttocks
against the yellow drawn shades,—

Who shall say I am not
the happy genius of my household?

WILLIAM CARLOS WILLIAMS WAS BORN IN RUTHERFORD, NEW JERSEY IN 1883. WHILE STUDYING TO BECOME A DOCTOR, HE BEFRIENDED EZRA POUND, WHO HELPED PUBLISH WILLIAMS' SECOND COLLECTION, THE TEMPERS. WILLIAMS SUSTAINED HIS MEDICAL PRACTICE THROUGHOUT HIS LIFE, THOUGH IS KNOWN FOR HIS MAJOR WORKS SUCH AS PICTURES FROM BRUEGHEL AND OTHER POEMS (1962), A NATIONAL BOOK AWARD FINALIST. WILLIAMS DIED IN 1963.

Faith

TERENCE WINCH

In the linoleum there are alligators
when his mother comes to him at night.
Inside the apartment is a long hall
that turns halfway, the mother walking
the hall holding onto the walls
so she will not fall. In her bed
she grows old, swells up,
hair grows on her like a man.
In the early hours of a dark mid-
December day, she begins to fail.

Outside, on the street, stands the convent.
The nuns entrap the children, trick
them into going to the A&P, invite
them into the parlor of the convent.
A whiskered nun stands on the
convent steps waiting to catch children
to run errands. An old nun keeps
the convent clean. She washes floors
and dishes, polishes old wood. She is
the nun's nun. The nuns cannot touch
each other, but they touch the children
when they can. There are small nuns,
fat nuns, nuns who play the piano,
queer nuns, singing and flying nuns,
old nuns, young nuns, dumb nuns,
fun nuns, attack nuns who smack and whack,
holy nuns who help the poor, sexy nuns
who know the score, departed nuns
we will see no more.

The best nuns of all are the Dominican
Sisters of the Sick Poor, who appear
every day at our door, each one a real
nurse, easing my mother's pain and fear
as she grows worse and worse
before she disappears and is seen no more
except in dreams, and even then
as a stranger on a distant shore
where we will sail to meet her
when the darkness is dispelled,
our souls opening like fists
our frail faith set free at last.

TERENCE WINCH IS THE AUTHOR OF THREE BOOKS OF POEMS, *THE DRIFT OF THINGS* (2001), *THE GREAT INDOORS* (1995) AND *IRISH MUSICIANS/AMERICAN FRIENDS* (1985), WHICH WON AN AMERICAN BOOK AWARD. ALSO A MUSICIAN AND SONGWRITER, WINCH RECORDED THREE ALBUMS, ALL FEATURING HIS COMPOSITIONS, WITH CELTIC THUNDER, AN IRISH BAND HE CO-FOUNDED IN 1977.

I first read William Carlos Williams' DANSE RUSSE as a young man, boy really, and thought I understood some important things about it, like his use of what appears to be conversational, prosey, vernacular "American" (but contains hidden rhymes and rhythms that scan etc.) to describe a moment that evokes the struggle to accept oneself and our essential loneliness and inevitable demise—the joy in despair, or despite it. Even as a boy, having grown up in a family of six kids and grandparents and boarders and others staying for various lengths of time in a small house, I knew what it was to be lonely despite living among plenty of others. But I knew little of what it meant to be "the head" of a household, responsible for its well-being at least on some levels, financially say, and once I did, the poem became even more rich, revealed more depth to its layers of meaning, the resonance of its cry from one lonely human to whomever might be listening in the night. FAITH evokes a similar sense of sadness at the inevitability of death, of loneliness in the face of the death of others, in this case his mother, representative of all those who gave life to us, who came before us, who tied us to the world of passing time, and when they left that world could comfort us only in memory and dreams. Both poems reaffirm a kind of faith in the moment, and in the acceptance of reality, which is the key to peace, and sometimes even joy.

-Michael Lally

ALIX
LAMBERT

TRACKS 12,13

Touch Me

STANLEY KUNITZ

Summer is late, my heart.
Words plucked out of the air
some forty years ago
when I was wild with love
and torn almost in two
scatter like leaves this night
of whistling wind and rain.
It is my heart that's late,
it is my song that's flown.
Outdoors all afternoon
under a gunmetal sky
staking my garden down,
I kneeled to the crickets trilling
underfoot as if about
to burst from their crusty shells;
and like a child again
marveled to hear so clear
and brave a music pour
from such a small machine.
What makes the engine go?
Desire, desire, desire.
The longing for the dance
stirs in the buried life.
One season only,
                    and it's done.
So let the battered old willow
thrash against the windowpanes
and the house timbers creak.
Darling, do you remember
the man you married? Touch me,
remind me who I am.

STANLEY KUNITZ WAS BORN IN WORCESTER, MASSACHUSETTS IN 1905. KUNITZ PUBLISHED HIS FIRST BOOK OF POETRY, *INTELLECTUAL THINGS,* IN 1930. DEEPLY COMMITTED TO FOSTERING COMMUNITY AMONG ARTISTS, HE WAS A FOUNDER OF THE FINE ARTS WORK CENTER IN PROVINCETOWN, MASSACHUSETTS, AND POETS HOUSE IN NEW YORK CITY. KUNITZ RECEIVED MANY HONORS FOR HIS POETRY WORKS, INCLUDING A NATIONAL BOOK AWARD, THE LENORE MARSHALL POETRY PRIZE, AND THE PULITZER PRIZE. HE ALSO SERVED AS UNITED STATES POET LAUREATE IN 2000. KUNITZ DIED AT THE AGE OF 100 IN 2006.

I remember meatloaf sandwiches made by Stanley, and his garden in Provincetown when I was a child, and the beginnings of our, often silent, communications thereafter. I was his great-niece. Years later, upon his reciting of TOUCH ME, I thought of Radnóti's LETTER TO MY WIFE, both of which make me feel something weepy and beautiful.

-Alix Lambert

Letter to My Wife

MIKLÓS RADNÓTI
TRANSLATED BY THOMAS LAND

Mute worlds lie in the depths, their stillness crying
inside my head; I shout: no-one's replying
in war-dazed, silenced Serbia the distant,
and you are far away. My dreams, persistent,
are woven nightly in your voice, and during
the day it's in my heart still reassuring—
and thus I keep my silence while, profoundly
detached, the cooling bracken stirs around me.

No longer can I guess when I will see you,
who were once firm and sure as psalms can be—you,
as lovely as the shadow and the light—you,
whom I could seek out mute, deprived of sight—you,
now with this landscape you don't know entwined—you,
projected to the eyes, but from the mind—you,
once real till to the realm of dreams you fell—you,
observed from my own puberty's deep well—you,

nagged jealously in my soul for a truthful
pledge that you love me, that upon the youthful
proud peak of life you'll be my bride; I'm yearning
and then, with sober consciousness returning,
I do remember that you are my wife and
my friend—past three wild frontiers, terrified land.
Will autumn leave me here forgotten, aching?
My memory is sharper over our lovemaking;

I once believed in miracles, forgetting
their time; above me, bomber squadrons setting
against the sky where I just watched the spark and
the colour of your eyes—the blue then darkened,
the bombs then longed to fall. I live despite them
and I am captive. I have weighed up, item
by painful item, all my hopes still tended—
and will yet find you. For you, I've descended,

along the highways, down the soul's appalling
deep chasms. I will project myself through falling
live flames or crimson coals to conquer the distance,
if need be learn the treebark's tough resistance—
the calm and might of fighting men whose power
in danger springs from cool appraisal shower
upon me, bringing sober strength anew,
and I become as calm as 2 x 2.

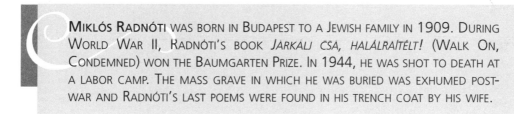

MIKLÓS RADNÓTI WAS BORN IN BUDAPEST TO A JEWISH FAMILY IN 1909. DURING WORLD WAR II, RADNÓTI'S BOOK *JARKALJ CSA, HALÁLRAÍTÉLT!* (WALK ON, CONDEMNED) WON THE BAUMGARTEN PRIZE. IN 1944, HE WAS SHOT TO DEATH AT A LABOR CAMP. THE MASS GRAVE IN WHICH HE WAS BURIED WAS EXHUMED POST-WAR AND RADNÓTI'S LAST POEMS WERE FOUND IN HIS TRENCH COAT BY HIS WIFE.

JOHN
LANDIS

TRACK 14

The War Prayer

MARK TWAIN

It was a time of great and exalting excitement.

The country was up in arms, the war was on, in every breast burned the holy fire of patriotism; the drums were beating, the bands playing, the toy pistols popping, the bunched firecrackers hissing and spluttering; on every hand and far down the receding and fading spread of roofs and balconies a fluttering wilderness of flags flashed in the sun; daily the young volunteers marched down the wide avenue gay and fine in their new uniforms, the proud fathers and mothers and sisters and sweethearts cheering them with voices choked with happy emotion as they swung by; nightly the packed mass meetings listened, panting, to patriot oratory which stirred the deepest deeps of their hearts, and which they interrupted at briefest intervals with cyclones of applause, the tears running down their cheeks the while; in the churches the pastors preached devotion to flag and country, and invoked the God of Battles beseeching His aid in our good cause in outpourings of fervid eloquence which moved every listener. It was indeed a glad and gracious time, and the half-dozen rash spirits that ventured to disapprove of the war and cast a doubt upon its righteousness straightway got such a stern and angry warning that for their personal safety's sake they quickly shrank out of sight and offended no more in that way.

Sunday morning came—next day the battalions would leave for the front; the church was filled; the volunteers were there, their young faces alight with martial dreams—visions of the stern advance, the gathering momentum, the rushing charge, the flashing sabers, the flight of the foe, the tumult, the enveloping smoke, the fierce pursuit, the surrender! Then home from the war, bronzed heroes, welcomed, adored, submerged in golden seas of glory! With the volunteers sat their dear ones, proud, happy, and envied by the neighbors and friends who had no sons and brothers to send forth to the field of honor, there to win for the flag, or, failing, die the noblest of noble deaths. The service proceeded; a war chapter from the Old Testament was read; the first prayer was said; it was followed by an organ burst that shook the building, and with one impulse the house rose, with glowing eyes and beating hearts, and poured out that tremendous invocation

God the all-terrible!
Thou who ordainest!
Thunder thy clarion
and lightning thy sword!

Then came the "long" prayer. None could remember the like of it for passionate pleading and moving and beautiful language. The burden of its supplication was, that an ever-merciful and benignant Father of us all would watch over our noble young soldiers, and aid, comfort, and encourage them in their patriotic work; bless them, shield them in the day of battle and the hour of peril, bear them in His mighty hand, make them strong and confident, invincible in the bloody onset; help them to crush the foe, grant to them and to their flag and country imperishable honor and glory—

An aged stranger entered and moved with slow and noiseless step up the main aisle, his eyes fixed upon the minister, his long body clothed in a robe that reached to his feet, his head bare, his white hair descending in a frothy cataract to his shoulders, his seamy face unnaturally pale, pale even to ghastliness. With all eyes following him and wondering, he made his silent way; without pausing, he ascended to the preacher's side and stood there waiting. With shut lids the preacher, unconscious of his presence, continued with his moving prayer, and at last finished it with the words, uttered in fervent appeal, "Bless our arms, grant us the victory, O Lord our God, Father and Protector of our land and flag!"

The stranger touched his arm, motioned him to step aside—which the startled minister did—and took his place. During some moments he surveyed the spell-bound audience with solemn eyes, in which burned an uncanny light; then in a deep voice he said:

"I come from the Throne—bearing a message from Almighty God!" The words smote the house with a shock; if the stranger perceived it he gave no attention. "He has heard the prayer of His servant your shepherd, and will grant it if such shall be your desire after I, His messenger, shall have explained to you its import—that is to say, its full import. For it is like unto many of the prayers of men, in that it asks for more than he who utters it is aware of—except he pause and think.

"God's servant and yours has prayed his prayer. Has he paused and taken thought? Is it one prayer? No, it is two—one uttered, the other not. Both have reached the ear of Him Who heareth all supplications, the spoken and the unspoken. Ponder this—keep it in mind. If you would beseech a blessing upon yourself, beware! Lest without intent you invoke a curse upon a neighbor at the same time. If you pray for the blessing of rain upon your crop which needs it, by that act you are possibly praying for a curse upon some neighbor's crop which may not need rain and can be injured by it.

"You have heard your servant's prayer—the uttered part of it. I am commissioned of God to put into words the other part of it—that part which the pastor—and also you in your hearts—fervently prayed silently. And ignorantly and unthinkingly? God grant that it was so! You heard these words: 'Grant us the victory, O Lord our God!' That is sufficient. the whole of the uttered prayer is compact into those pregnant words. Elaborations were not necessary. When you have prayed for victory you have prayed for many unmentioned results which follow victory— must follow it, cannot help but follow it. Upon the listening spirit of God fell also the unspoken part of the prayer. He commandeth me to put it into words. Listen!

"O Lord our Father, our young patriots, idols of our hearts, go forth to battle—be Thou near them! With them—in spirit—we also go forth from the sweet peace of our beloved firesides to smite the foe.
O Lord our God,
Help us to tear their soldiers to bloody shreds with our shells;
Help us to cover their smiling fields with the pale forms of their patriot dead;
Help us to drown the thunder of the guns with the shrieks of their wounded, writhing in pain;
Help us to lay waste their humble homes with a hurricane of fire;
Help us to wring the hearts of their unoffending widows with unavailing grief;
Help us to turn them out roofless with little children to wander unfriended the wastes of their desolated land in rags and hunger and thirst,
Sports of the sun flames of summer and the icy winds of winter,
Broken in spirit,
Worn with travail,
Imploring Thee for the refuge of the grave and denied it—
For our sakes who adore Thee, Lord,
Blast their hopes,
Blight their lives,
Protract their bitter pilgrimage,
Make heavy their steps,
Water their way with their tears,

Stain the white snow with the blood of their wounded feet!
We ask it, in the spirit of love,
Of Him Who is the Source of Love, and Who is the ever-faithful refuge and friend of all that
are sore beset and seek His aid with humble and contrite hearts.
Amen."

"Ye have prayed it; if ye still desire it, speak!—The messenger of the Most High waits!"

It was believed afterward that the man was a lunatic, because there was no sense in what he said.

MARK TWAIN WAS THE PEN NAME OF SAMUEL LANGHORNE CLEMENS, BORN IN 1835, AN AMERICAN HUMORIST, SATIRIST, LECTURER, AND WRITER. ON A VOYAGE TO NEW ORLEANS DOWN THE MISSISSIPPI, TWAIN WAS INSPIRED TO PURSUE A CAREER AS A STEAMBOAT PILOT WHICH PROVIDED MUCH OF THE MATERIAL FOR HIS MOST NOTED NOVELS, *THE ADVENTURES OF HUCKLEBERRY FINN* AND *THE ADVENTURES OF TOM SAWYER.*

"I believe that our heavenly father invented man because he was disappointed in the monkey." —Mark Twain

My admiration for Samuel Langhorne Clemens, for who he was and what he became, for where he came from and who he evolved into, has no limits. Since my first time reading THE ADVENTURES OF HUCKLEBERRY FINN when I was eleven years old, my relationship with Mark Twain remains profound. His writings and force of personality continue to influence me.

When Jason Shinder asked me to come up with a poem "important to me", I thought long and hard. The title verse in Twain's short story THE WAR PRAYER is what I've chosen for its power and relevance to the world today. Prayer has always been poetry and in this prayer for victory Mark Twain wants us to understand exactly what we are praying for. President George W. Bush, Vice President Dick Cheney, Condoleezza Rice, and the others in this the most dishonest, corrupt, and incompetent administration in our country's history, have embroiled us in an imperialist military action with no end in sight. Mark Twain's words ring true.

-John Landis

MELISSA LEO

TRACKS 15,16

Point Shirley
SYLVIA PLATH

From Water-Tower Hill to the brick prison
The shingle booms, bickering under
The sea's collapse.
Snowcakes break and welter. This year
The gritted wave leaps
The seawall and drops onto a bier
Of quahog chips,
Leaving a salty mash of ice to whiten

In my grandmother's sand yard. She is dead,
Whose laundry snapped and froze here, who
Kept house against
What the sluttish, rutted sea could do.
Squall waves once danced
Ship timbers in through the cellar window;
A thresh-tailed, lanced
Shark littered in the geranium bed–

Such collusion of mulish elements
She wore her broom straws to the nub.
Twenty years out
Of her hand, the house still hugs in each drab
Stucco socket
The purple egg-stones: from Great Head's knob
To the filled-in Gut
The sea in its cold gizzard ground those rounds.

Nobody wintering now behind
The planked-up windows where she set
Her wheat loves
And apple cakes to cool. What is it
Survives, grieves
So, over this battered, obstinate spit
Of gravel? The waves'
Spewed relics clicker masses in the wind,

Grey waves the stub-necked eiders ride.
A labor of love, and that labor lost.
Steadily the sea
Eats at Point Shirley. She died blessed,
And I come by
Bones, bones only, pawed and tossed,
A dog-faced sea.
The sun sinks under Boston, bloody red.

I would get from these dry-papped stones
The milk your love instilled in them.
The black ducks dive.
And through your graciousness might stream,
And I contrive,
Grandmother, stones are nothing of home
To that spumiest dove.
Against both bar and tower the black sea turns.

SYLVIA PLATH WAS BORN IN BOSTON, MASSACHUSETTS, 1932. IN 1962, PLATH WROTE MOST OF THE POEMS THAT WOULD COMPRISE HER MOST FAMOUS BOOK, *ARIEL*, AND IN 1963, SHE PUBLISHED A SEMI-AUTOBIOGRAPHICAL NOVEL, *THE BELL JAR*, UNDER A PSEUDONYM. SHE COMMITTED SUICIDE IN 1963. PLATH'S *THE COLLECTED POEMS*, PUBLISHED POSTHUMOUSLY, WON A PULITZER PRIZE IN 1982.

Sonnet 64

WILLIAM SHAKESPEARE

When I have seen by Time's fell hand defaced
The rich, proud cost of outworn buried age;
When sometime lofty towers I see down-razed
And brass eternal slave to mortal rage;
When I have seen the hungry ocean gain
Advantage on the kingdom of the shore,
And the firm soil win of the watery main,
Increasing store with loss and loss with store;
When I have seen such interchange of state,
Or state itself confounded to decay:
Ruin hath taught me thus to ruminate,
That Time will come and take my love away.
    This thought is as a death, which cannot choose
    But weep to have that which it fears to lose.

WILLIAM SHAKESPEARE WAS BORN IN 1564 IN STRATFORD-ON-AVON. IN 1594, SHAKESPEARE JOINED THE LORD CHAMBERLAIN'S COMPANY OF ACTORS, THE MOST POPULAR COMPANY ACTING AT COURT. SHAKESPEARE'S SONNETS WERE COMPOSED BETWEEN 1593 AND 1601, THOUGH THEY WERE NOT PUBLISHED UNTIL 1609 AS *THE SONNETS OF SHAKESPEARE* CONSISTING OF 154 SONNETS. HE DIED IN 1616.

I first found both of my selections in my early twenties as an acting
major at SUNY Purchase. We each chose a sonnet and used it in voice
speech and acting classes in our first year. "When I have seen by Time's fell
hand..." had the observation of decay that even as a young woman I had
an awareness of. The clarity of it has only enriched over time.
Accessibility is very important to me in any reading matter.
My acting mentor, Joan Potter, lead me to Sylvia Plath. The dark brilliant
poetess who did herself in. Mad? Perhaps...I was hooked. POINT SHIRLEY
is entirely evocative of the Springs, N.Y. where I have spent time since I
was five. The narrow strip of road where Accabonac Harbor almost
touches Gardiner's Bay is my Point Shirley. Yesterday I read the poem to
my 93 year old grandmother as she lay in the ICU in South Hampton
Hospital. Plath's line about her grandmother's broom drew a chuckle from
Elinore who remarked on the great power of wordsmiths.

-Melissa Leo

JOHN LITHGOW

The Lake Isle at Innisfree

W. B. YEATS

I will arise and go now, and go to Innisfree,
And a small cabin build there, of clay and wattles made:
Nine bean-rows will I have there, a hive for the honey-bee,
And live alone in the bee-loud glade.

And I shall have some peace there, for peace comes dropping slow,
Dropping from the veils of the morning to where the cricket sings;
There midnight's all a glimmer, and noon a purple glow,
And evening full of the linnet's wings.

I will arise and go now, for always night and day
I hear lake water lapping with low sounds by the shore;
While I stand on the roadway, or on the pavements grey,
I hear it in the deep heart's core.

W. B. YEATS WAS BORN IN DUBLIN, IRELAND, IN 1865. DEEPLY INVOLVED IN IRELAND'S POLITICS, HIS VERSE REFLECTED PESSIMISM ABOUT HIS COUNTRY'S POLITICAL SITUATION. AS A SENATOR OF THE IRISH FREE STATE IN 1922, HE WAS AN IMPORTANT CULTURAL LEADER AND A MAJOR PLAYWRIGHT, CO-FOUNDING THE FAMOUS ABBEY THEATRE IN DUBLIN. YEATS WAS AWARDED THE NOBEL PRIZE IN 1923 AND DIED IN 1939.

To Autumn

JOHN KEATS

I.

Season of mists and mellow fruitfulness,
  Close bosom-friend of the maturing sun;
Conspiring with him how to load and bless
  With fruit the vines that round the thatch-eves run;
To bend with apples the moss'd cottage-trees,
  And fill all fruit with ripeness to the core;
    To swell the gourd, and plump the hazel shells
  With a sweet kernel; to set budding more,
And still more, later flowers for the bees,
Until they think warm days will never cease,
    For Summer has o'er-brimm'd their clammy cells.

II.

Who hath not seen thee oft amid thy store?
  Sometimes whoever seeks abroad may find
Thee sitting careless on a granary floor
  Thy hair soft-lifted by the winnowing wind;
Or on a half-reap'd furrow sound asleep,
  Drows'd with the fume of poppies, while thy hook
    Spares the next swath and all its twined flowers:
And sometimes like a gleaner thou dost keep
  Steady thy laden head across a brook;
  Or by a cider-press, with patient look,
    Thou watchest the last oozings hours by hours.

III.

Where are the songs of Spring? Ay, where are they?
  Think not of them, thou hast thy music too,—
    While barred clouds bloom the soft-dying day,
And touch the stubble-plains with rosy hue;
  Then in a wailful choir the small gnats mourn
  Among the river sallows, borne aloft

Or sinking as the light wind lives or dies;
And full-grown lambs loud bleat from hilly bourn;
Hedge-crickets sing; and now with treble soft
The red-breast whistles from a garden-croft;
And gathering swallows twitter in the skies.

JOHN KEATS WAS BORN IN LONDON IN 1795. IN 1818, HE FELL IN LOVE WITH A WOMAN NAMED FANNY BRAWNE AND WROTE SOME OF HIS FINEST POETRY OVER THE NEXT YEAR. BY THE AGE OF 23, HE CONTRACTED TUBERCULOSIS BUT MANAGED TO PUBLISH HIS THIRD VOLUME OF POETRY, *LAMIA, ISABELLA, THE EVE OF ST. AGNES, AND OTHER POEMS,* TWO YEARS LATER. KEATS DIED IN 1821.

I've always found Yeats' THE LAKE ISLE AT INNISFREE to be the most comforting and at the same time the most melancholy of poems. It is perfectly serene and yet it is all about the longing for serenity. I read it aloud at the memorial service for Joseph Maher, an actor whom every actor adored. It was the right choice to memorialize an Irishman—full of sadness at his passing but relief at his finding rest. Keats' TO AUTUMN is one of the only poems I actually sat down and memorized. It was during my college years in New England, a part of the country where autumn is especially ripe and evocative. At that age, in that place, and at that time of year, I was full to bursting with autumnal feelings. In the golden season of harvest, on the verge of a bitter, cold winter, with springtime a far-off hope, the Romantic poets spoke to me then more urgently than they've ever spoken to me since.

–John Lithgow

BILLY LUTHER

White Shell Ever-Changing Woman

SUNNY DOOLEY

Atop Chol II
At the purest edge of darkness
At the purest start of light
Mists of sky and mists of earth
Embraced
As clouds of white, blue, abalone and jet swirled
From east to west
From north to south
Unfurled ribbons of rainbows crossed
Beneath its arch
Taking sacred breath was a child
Resting on all the essences of what is all of earth and
what is all of sky
nourished on dewdrops and pollens
She stood on turquoise
Stepped into her white shell moccasins of endurance
She wrapped blue velvet clouds around her
Upon it she placed the mountains, rivers, streams and cloud vapors
She belted her waist with the rainbow
On her wrist and neck she placed laces of swirling clouds of white shell, turquoise,
Abalone and jet

She took a grass brush
Began to comb her hair that lay as sprays of rain and fragrant blossoms
She combed into each strand every subtle nuance of grace, strength, charm and
Wisdom
Wrapped it into a bundle at the nape of her neck
tied it with sunbeams
She stood
Illuminated?
This Whiteshell-Ever-Changing-Woman
When she spoke
It was
Ho zho jii

SUNNY DOOLEY IS A DINE' (NAVAJO) STORYTELLER, POET, AND FOLK SINGER. THE FORMER MISS NAVAJO BEAUTY PAGEANT WINNER WAS BORN IN THE CHI CHIL' TAH COMMUNITY IN NEW MEXICO, AND CURRENTLY TRAVELS THE WORLD SHARING STORIES THAT HAVE BEEN PASSED DOWN FOR GENERATIONS IN HER FAMILY.

When I was making a film about the Miss Navajo Nation beauty pageant, I was also focusing on the theme of women in Navajo culture. Since this was a pageant that showcased the skills and talents of traditional Navajo women, I knew I wanted to explore the role of our female deity—Changing Woman.

I had asked former Miss Navajo, Sunny Dooley, to write a poem about Changing Woman to be included in the film. When she presented me with her final draft, I was awestruck. How could she have captured everything that Miss Navajo Nation and we as Navajo people strive for in such a short poem?

I was extremely fortunate to have her words included in my film. People request this poem wherever I travel with the film. It inspires me to continue to improve everyday as a Navajo, a filmmaker, and an artist.
-Billy Luther

from On The Pulse of Morning

MAYA ANGELOU

A Rock, A River, A Tree
Hosts to species long since departed,
Mark the mastodon.
The dinosaur, who left dry tokens
Of their sojourn here
On our planet floor,
Any broad alarm of their of their hastening doom
Is lost in the gloom of dust and ages.

But today, the Rock cries out to us, clearly, forcefully,
Come, you may stand upon my
Back and face your distant destiny,
But seek no haven in my shadow.
I will give you no hiding place down here.

You, created only a little lower than
The angels, have crouched too long in
The bruising darkness,
Have lain too long
Facedown in ignorance.
Your mouths spelling words
Armed for slaughter.

The Rock cries out today,
You may stand on me,
But do not hide your face.

MAYA ANGELOU, BORN IN ST. LOUIS IN 1928, IS A POET AND PERFORMER. SHE HAS RECEIVED NATIONAL BOOK AWARD AND PULITZER PRIZE NOMINATIONS FOR HER WRITING AND TONY AWARD NOMINATIONS FOR HER ACTING. ANGELOU HAS WRITTEN FOR PUBLICATIONS AROUND THE WORLD, INCLUDING EGYPT AND AFRICA, AND DELIVERED HER POEM, *ON THE PULSE OF MORNING*, AT PRESIDENT BILL CLINTON'S INAUGURATION, AT HIS REQUEST.

I was 17 years old when I first heard Maya Angelou read this poem. And before then, there wasn't a poem that resonated with me. It's hard to express in words what this means to me. History and Humanity?

-Billy Luther

PETER
MACNICOL

}TRACKS 17,18

Sea Fever

JOHN MASEFIELD

I must go down to the seas again,
to the lonely sea and the sky,
And all I ask is a tall ship
and a star to steer her by;
And the wheel's kick and the wind's song
and the white sail's shaking,
And a grey mist on the sea's face, and
a grey dawn breaking,

I must down to the seas again,
for the call of the running tide
Is a wild call and a clear call
that may not be denied; And all I ask is a windy day
with the white clouds flying,
And the flung spray and the blown spume,
and the sea-gulls crying.

I must down to the seas again,
to the vagrant gypsy life,
To the gull's way and the whale's way
where the wind's like a whetted knife;
And all I ask is a merry yarn
from a laughing fellow-rover,
And quiet sleep and a sweet dream
when the long trick's over.

JOHN MASEFIELD WAS BORN IN LEDBURY, ENGLAND IN 1878. AFTER THE DEATH OF BOTH PARENTS, MASEFIELD WAS SENT TO A SEA-CADET SHIP TO TRAIN FOR A LIFE AT SEA. BY THE TIME HE WAS 21, HIS POEM, *NICIAS MORITURAS* WAS PUBLISHED, AND HE DISCOVERED THE POETRY OF W.B. YEATS AND MET THE FAMOUS POET, WHICH RESULTED IN A LIFELONG FRIENDSHIP. IN 1912, HE WON THE THE EDMUND DE POLIGNAC PRIZE. MASEFIELD WAS NAMED POET LAUREATE IN 1930, A POSITION HE HELD UNTIL HIS DEATH IN 1967.

Song of Enchantment

WALTER DE LA MARE

A Song of Enchantment I sang me there,
In a green—green wood, by waters fair,
Just as the words came up to me
I sang it under the wildwood tree.

Widdershins turned I, singing it low,
Watching the wild birds come and go;
No cloud in the deep dark blue to be seen
Under the thick-thatched branches green.

Twilight came; silence came;
The planet of Evening's silver flame;
By darkening paths I wandered through
Thickets trembling with drops of dew.

But the music is lost and the words are gone
Of the song I sang as I sat alone,
Ages and ages have fallen on me—
On the wood and the pool and the elder tree.

WALTER DE LA MARE WAS BORN IN KENT, ENGLAND IN 1873. DE LA MARE'S THE LISTENERS (1912) WAS HIS FIRST WIDELY SUCCESSFUL BOOK AND THE TITLE POEM IS ONE OF HIS MOST ANTHOLOGIZED PIECES. HIS 1921 NOVEL. MEMOIRS OF A MIDGET, WON THE JAMES TAIT BLACK MEMORIAL PRIZE FOR FICTION. HE DIED IN 1953.

It seems to not matter that John Masefield was chosen poet laureate in preference to several of the most luminous names in the history of British verse, names like A. E. Housman, Rudyard Kipling, Walter De La Mare, and Masefield's own mentor, W.B. Yeats, no matter that he remained England's national poet all the way to his death in 1967, making him second only to Tennyson in length of service as laureate. It's equally no matter that Robert Graves called him "his hero" or that schoolchildren throughout the English-speaking world commited his most famous poems to memory. Poems like SEA FEVER and CARGOES will be around two hundred years from now. Just don't look for them in the most recent Nortons' Anthology or at Borders or Barnes & Noble. I suppose his style is too unsubtle, too musical, too cadenced and comprehensible for today's campus critics. A sad thing, snobbery, but there it is.

I memorized SEA FEVER and other Masefield poems back when I was a seventh grader at Crockett Junior High School. I could either stare out the window on the living museum of mundanity that was my hometown or I could open a book and be up and away, traveling with the trade winds across Spanish Seas or dreaming of "distant Ophir." Masefield's poems were faraway ports-of-call and left me word-drunk and world-wanting.

-Peter MacNicol

MATTHEW MAHER

TRACKS 19,20

The Song of Wandering Aengus

W. B. YEATS

I went out to the hazel wood,
Because a fire was in my head,
And cut and peeled a hazel wand,
And hooked a berry to a thread;
And when white moths were on the wing,
And moth-like stars were flickering out,
I dropped the berry in a stream
And caught a little silver trout.

When I had laid it on the floor
I went to blow the fire aflame,
But something rustled on the floor,
And some one called me by my name:
It had become a glimmering girl
With apple blossom in her hair
Who called me by my name and ran
And faded through the brightening air.

Though I am old with wandering
Through hollow lands and hilly lands,
I will find out where she has gone,
And kiss her lips and take her hands;
And walk among long dappled grass,
And pluck till time and times are done
The silver apples of the moon,
The golden apples of the sun.

The Invisible Men

NAKASAK
TRANSLATED BY EDWARD FIELD

There is a tribe of invisible men
Who move around us like shadows—have you felt them?
They have bodies like ours and live just like us,
Using the same weapons and tools.
You can see their tracks in the snow sometimes
And even their igloos
But never the invisible men themselves.
They cannot be seen except when they die
For then they become visible.

It once happened that a human woman
Married one of the invisible men.
He was a good husband in every way:
He went out hunting and brought her food,
And they could talk together like any other couple.
But the wife could not bear the thought
That she did not know what the man she married looked like.
One day when they were both at home
She was so overcome with curiosity to see him
That she stabbed with a knife where she knew he was sitting.
And her desire was fulfilled:
Before her eyes a handsome young man fell to the floor.
But he was cold and dead, and too late
She realized what she had done,
And sobbed her heart out.

When the invisible men heard about this murder
They came out of their igloos to take revenge.
Their bows were seen moving through the air
And the bowstrings stretching as they aimed their arrows.
The humans stood there helplessly
For they had no idea what to do or how to fight
Because they could not see their assailants.
But the invisible men had a code of honor
That forbade them to attack opponents
Who could not defend themselves,
So they did not let their arrows fly,
And nothing happened; there was no battle after all
And everyone went back to their ordinary lives.

NAKASAK WAS A MEMBER OF THE INUIT TRIBE, BORN IN NORTHERN CANADA IN THE EARLY 1900S. HE HELPED THE U.S. NAVY FIND A SUITABLE AIRBASE LOCATION IN THE COMMUNITY NOW KNOWN AS IQALUIT, CANADA, IN THE 1940S.

I first read THE SONG OF WANDERING AENGUS when I was in college, and I loved it, of course. I can't think of another poem that so perfectly summed up and romanticized the longing—for love, for art, for freedom, or for the ideas of those things—that I felt when I was young. What's more, the poem seems to say that the longing for love, art, freedom, or any other longing one might identify with are all the same longing, and that this longing—more than the satisfaction of the longing—is the key to a full life. At 19, I would read it and feel crushed and exalted all at once: desperate to experience life, yet also feeling like I had figured life out, somehow. I'm 36 now, old enough to know how little I knew when I was

19, but not much else—but I still love the poem, and I still identify with it fiercely, and I hope I do all through my life. I guess it's possible to have experienced love, art and freedom, and still long for them. Anyway, when I was in college I saw the speaker as a young man wise beyond his years; now I see it as the song of a man who's lived many years, many lives, and is still young. Who knows what the poem will mean to me when I'm 80, but right now, it's a lesson, a prayer, and a reminder.

I came across the THE INVISIBLE MEN recently. In fact, in looking for the poem for this book, I had upturned my library, and the more I looked for it, the more indistinct my memory of the poem itself became. I was not even sure for a moment if the poem actually existed—perhaps it was an amalgamation of a bunch of different poems I'd read over the years—or a memory of reading a poem, with the poem itself no longer a part of the memory. It's an invisible poem, basically, that led me to "The Invisible Men", which I encountered while flipping through an anthology, having all but given up on my search. I've read it over a dozen times since, and I'm sure I'll keep returning to it. It takes on a different meaning, a different tone, every time I read it; or rather, the meanings seem to divide and multiply within themselves, the poem becoming more specific and mysterious as I go. The poem itself is like the invisible men of the story— varied and unknowable, like ordinary life.

-Matthew Maher

WALTER
MOSLEY

Lying in a Hammock at William Duffy's Farm in Pine Island, Minnesota

JAMES WRIGHT

Over my head, I see the bronze butterfly,
Asleep on the black trunk,
blowing like a leaf in green shadow.
Down the ravine behind the empty house,
The cowbells follow one another
Into the distances of the afternoon.
To my right,
In a field of sunlight between two pines,
The droppings of last year's horses
Blaze up into golden stones.
I lean back, as the evening darkens and comes on.
A chicken hawk floats over, looking for home.
I have wasted my life.

JAMES WRIGHT WAS BORN IN MARTINS FERRY, OHIO, 1927. HE USED HIS POETRY AS A MODE TO DISCUSS HIS POLITICAL AND SOCIAL CONCERNS, PARTICULARLY IN HIS EARLIER BOOKS, SUCH AS THE GREEN WALL (1957), WINNER OF THE YALE SERIES OF YOUNGER POETS AWARD. WRIGHT RECEIVED THE PULITZER PRIZE IN POETRY FOR HIS COLLECTED POEMS IN 1972. HE DIED IN 1980.

The Sundays of Satin-Legs Smith

GWENDOLYN BROOKS

Inamoratas, with an approbation,
Bestowed his title. Blessed his inclination.

He wakes, unwinds, elaborately: a cat
Tawny, reluctant, royal. He is fat
And fine this morning. Definite. Reimbursed.

He waits a moment, he designs his reign,
That no performance may be plain or vain.
Then rises in a clear delirium.

He sheds, with his pajamas, shabby days.
And his desertedness, his intricate fear, the
Postponed resentments and the prim precautions.

Now, at his bath, would you deny him lavender
Or take away the power of his pine?
What smelly substitute, heady as wine,
Would you provide? life must be aromatic.
There must be scent, somehow there must be some.
Would you have flowers in his life? suggest
Asters? a Really Good geranium?
A white carnation? would you prescribe a Show
With the cold lilies, formal chrysanthemum
Magnificence, poinsettias, and emphatic
Red of prize roses? might his happiest
Alternative (you muse) be, after all,
A bit of gentle garden in the best
Of taste and straight tradition? Maybe so.
But you forget, or did you ever know,
His heritage of cabbage and pigtails,
Old intimacy with alleys, garbage pails,
Down in the deep (but always beautiful) South
Where roses blush their blithest (it is said)
And sweet magnolias put Chanel to shame.

No! He has not a flower to his name.
Except a feather one, for his lapel.
Apart from that, if he should think of flowers
It is in terms of dandelions or death.
Ah, there is little hope. You might as well—
Unless you care to set the world a-boil
And do a lot of equalizing things,
Remove a little ermine, say, from kings,
Shake hands with paupers and appoint them men,
For instance—certainly you might as well
Leave him his lotion, lavender and oil.

Let us proceed. Let us inspect, together
With his meticulous and serious love,
The innards of this closet. Which is a vault
Whose glory is not diamonds, not pearls,
Not silver plate with just enough dull shine.
But wonder-suits in yellow and in wine,
Sarcastic green and zebra-striped cobalt.
With shoulder padding that is wide
And cocky and determined as his pride;
Ballooning pants that taper off to ends
Scheduled to choke precisely.
                            Here are hats
Like bright umbrellas; and hysterical ties
Like narrow banners for some gathering war.

People are so in need, in need of help.
People want so much that they do not know.

Below the tinkling trade of little coins
The gold impulse not possible to show
Or spend. Promise piled over and betrayed.

These kneaded limbs receive the kiss of silk.
Then they receive the brave and beautiful
Embrace of some of that equivocal wool.
He looks into his mirror, loves himself—

The neat curve here; the angularity
That is appropriate at just its place;
The technique of a variegated grace.

Here is all his sculpture and his art
And all his architectural design.
Perhaps you would prefer to this a fine
Value of marble, complicated stone.
Would have him think with horror of baroque,
Rococo. You forget and you forget.

He dances down the hotel steps that keep
Remnants of last night's high life and distress.
As spat-out purchased kisses and spilled beer.
He swallows sunshine with a secret yelp.
Passes to coffee and a roll or two.
Has breakfasted.
     Out. Sounds about him smear,
Become a unit. He hears and does not hear
The alarm clock meddling in somebody's sleep;
Children's governed Sunday happiness;
The dry tone of a plane; a woman's oath;
Consumption's spiritless expectoration;
An indignant robin's resolute donation
Pinching a track through apathy and din;
Restaurant vendors weeping; and the L
That comes on like a slightly horrible thought.

Pictures, too, as usual, are blurred.
He sees and does not see the broken windows
Hiding their shame with newsprint; little girl
With ribbons decking wornness, little boy
Wearing the trousers with the decentest patch,
To honor Sunday; women on their way
From "service" temperate holiness arranged
Ably on asking faces; men estranged
From music and from wonder and from joy
But far familiar with the guiding awe

Of foodlessness.
           He loiters.
                   Restaurant vendors
Weep, or out of them rolls a restless glee.
The Lonesome Blues, the Long-lost Blues, I Want A
Big Fat Mama. Down these sore avenues
Comes no Saint-Saëns, no piquant elusive Grieg,
And not Tschaikovsky's wayward eloquence
And not the shapely tender drift of Brahms.
But could he love them? Since a man must bring
To music what his mother spanked him for
When he was two: bits of forgotten hate,
Devotion: whether or not his mattress hurts:
The little dream his father humored: the thing
His sister did for money: what he ate
For breakfast—and for dinner twenty years
Ago last autumn: all his skipped desserts.

The pasts of his ancestors lean against
Him. Crowd him. Fog out his identity.
Hundreds of hungers mingle with his own,
Hundreds of voices advise so dexterously
He quite considers his reactions his,
Judges he walks most powerfully alone,
That everything is—simply what it is.

But movie-time approaches, time to boo
The hero's kiss, and boo the heroine
Whose ivory and yellow it is sin
For his eye to eat of. The Mickey Mouse,
However, is for everyone in the house.

Squires his lady to dinner at Joe's Eats.
His lady alters as to leg and eye,
Thickness and height, such minor points as these,
From Sunday to Sunday. But no matter what
Her name or body positively she's
In Queen Lace stockings with ambitious heels

That strain to kiss the calves, and vivid shoes
Frontless and backless, Chinese fingernails,
Earrings, three layers of lipstick, intense hat
Dripping with the most voluble of veils.
Her affable extremes are like sweet bombs
About him, whom no middle grace or good
Could gratify. He had no education
In quiet arts of compromise. He would
Not understand your counsels on control, nor
Thank you for your late trouble.

At Joe's Eats

You get your fish or chicken on meat platters.
With coleslaw, macaroni, candied sweets,
Coffee and apple pie. You go out full.
(The end is—isn't it?—all that really matters.)

And even and intrepid come
The tender boots of night to home.

Her body is like new brown bread
Under the Woolworth mignonette.
Her body is a honey bowl
Whose waiting honey is deep and hot.
Her body is like summer earth,
Receptive, soft, and absolute...

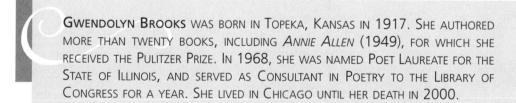

GWENDOLYN BROOKS WAS BORN IN TOPEKA, KANSAS IN 1917. SHE AUTHORED MORE THAN TWENTY BOOKS, INCLUDING *ANNIE ALLEN* (1949), FOR WHICH SHE RECEIVED THE PULITZER PRIZE. IN 1968, SHE WAS NAMED POET LAUREATE FOR THE STATE OF ILLINOIS, AND SERVED AS CONSULTANT IN POETRY TO THE LIBRARY OF CONGRESS FOR A YEAR. SHE LIVED IN CHICAGO UNTIL HER DEATH IN 2000.

TIM BLAKE NELSON

TRACKS 21,22

For The Union Dead

ROBERT LOWELL

Relinquunt Omnia Servare Rem Publicam.

The old South Boston Aquarium stands
in a Sahara of snow now. Its broken windows are boarded.
The bronze weathervane cod has lost half its scales.
The airy tanks are dry.

Once my nose crawled like a snail on the glass;
my hand tingled
to burst the bubbles,
drifting from the noses of the crowded, compliant fish.

My hand draws back. I often sigh still
for the dark downward and vegetating kingdom
of the fish and reptile. One morning last March,
I pressed against the new barbed and galvanized

fence on the Boston Common. Behind their cage,
yellow dinosaur steam shovels were grunting
as they cropped up tons of mush and grass
to gouge their underworld garage.

Parking spaces luxuriate like civic
sand piles in the heart of Boston.
a girdle of orange, Puritan-pumpkin-colored girders
braces the tingling Statehouse, shaking

over the excavations, as it faces Colonel Shaw
and his bell-cheeked Negro infantry
on St. Gaudens' shaking Civil War relief,
propped by a plank splint against the garage's earthquake.

Two months after marching through Boston,
half of the regiment was dead;
at the dedication,
William James could almost hear the bronze Negroes breathe.
The monument sticks like a fishbone
in the city's throat.
Its colonel is as lean
as a compass needle.

He has an angry wrenlike vigilance,
a greyhound's gentle tautness;
he seems to wince at pleasure
and suffocate for privacy.

He is out of bounds. He rejoices in man's lovely,
peculiar power to choose life and die —
when he leads his black soldiers to death,
he cannot bend his back.

On a thousand small-town New England greens
the old white churches hold their air
of sparse, sincere rebellion; frayed flags
quilt the graveyards of the Grand Army of the Republic

The stone statutes of the abstract Union Soldier
grow slimmer and younger each year —
wasp-waisted, they doze over muskets
and muse through their sideburns.

Shaw's father wanted no monument
except the ditch,
where his son's body was thrown
and lost with his "niggers."

The ditch is nearer.
There are no statues for the last war here;
on Boylston Street, a commercial photograph
shows Hiroshima boiling

over a Mosler Safe, the "Rock of Ages,"
that survived the blast. Space is nearer.
when I crouch to my television set,
the drained faces of Negro school-children rise like balloons.

Colonel Shaw
is riding on his bubble,
he waits
for the blessed break.

The Aquarium is gone. Everywhere,
giant finned cars nose forward like fish;
a savage servility
slides by on grease.

ROBERT LOWELL WAS BORN IN 1917 IN BOSTON. HIS FIRST AND SECOND BOOKS,
LAND OF UNLIKENESS AND *LORD WEARY'S CASTLE*, A PULITZER PRIZE WINNER,
EXPLORED THE DARK SIDE OF AMERICA'S PURITAN LEGACY. LOWELL SERVED AS A
CHANCELLOR OF THE ACADEMY OF AMERICAN POETS FROM 1962 UNTIL HIS DEATH
FROM A HEART ATTACK IN 1977.

*This poem, which I first encountered in the ninth grade in Tulsa,
Oklahoma, shows how images can be organized in a way that is utterly
rhetorical but without abstraction. While never straying from the
concrete, its accumulated power soars into a poignant argument about
history becoming submerged in a relentless and irresponsible present.*

-Tim Blake Nelson

Death Fugue

Paul Celan
Translated By Michael Hamburger

Black milk of daybreak we drink it at sundown
we drink it at noon in the morning we drink it at night
we drink and we drink it
we dig a grave in the breezes there one lies unconfined
A man lives in the house he plays with the serpents he writes
he writes when dusk falls to Germany your golden hair Margarete
he writes it and steps out of doors and the stars are flashing he whistles his pack out
he whistles his Jews out in earth has them dig for a grave
he commands us strike up for the dance

Black milk of daybreak we drink you at night
we drink in the morning at noon we drink you at sundown
we drink and we drink you
A man lives in the house he plays with the serpents he writes
he writes when dusk falls to Germany your golden hair Margarete
your ashen hair Shulamith we dig a grave in the breezes there one lies unconfined

He calls out jab deeper into the earth you lot you others sing now and play
he grabs at the iron in his belt he waves it his eyes are blue
jab deeper you lot with your spades you others play on for the dance

Black milk of daybreak we drink you at night
we drink you at noon in the morning we drink you at sundown
we drink and we drink you
a man lives in the house your golden hair Margarete
your ashen hair Shulamith he plays with the serpents

He calls out more sweetly play death death is a master from Germany
he calls out more darkly now stroke your strings then as smoke you will rise into air
then a grave you will have in the clouds there one lies unconfined

Black milk of daybreak we drink you at night
we drink you at noon death is a master from Germany
we drink you at sundown and in the morning we drink and we drink you
death is a master from Germany his eyes are blue
he strikes you with leaden bullets his aim is true
a man lives in the house your golden hair Margarete
he sets his pack on to us he grants us a grave in the air
he plays with the serpents and daydreams death is a master from Germany

> your golden hair Margarete
> your ashen hair Shulamith

PAUL CELAN WAS BORN IN CZERNOVITZ, ROMANIA IN 1920. CELAN'S INTERNMENT IN FORCED LABOR CAMPS DURING WORLD WAR II INFLUENCED HIS POETRY, INCLUDING *TODESFUGE* (DEATH FUGUE) IN HIS SECOND BOOK, *MOHN UND GEDAECHTNIS* (*POPPY AND MEMORY*), WHICH GARNERED TREMENDOUS ACCLAIM. HE PUBLISHED MORE THAN SIX BOOKS OF POETRY AND RECEIVED A GEORG BUCHNER PRIZE. IN 1970, CELAN COMMITTED SUICIDE.

Paul Celan, a holocaust survivor and defining modernist, wrote a devastatingly emotional poem with a prayer-like cadence that seizes and does not let go. I first read this while researching for The Grey Zone, and was astounded by its odd restraint and its uncompromising imagery. Celan's verse is swirlingly aggressive and never self-pitying. The poem is at once political and laceratingly personal. In but a few lines, he accomplishes a comprehensive power few have acheived in describing any human atrocity.
-Tim Blake Nelson

MICHAEL O'KEEFE

TRACKS 23,24

In a Station at the Metro

EZRA POUND

The apparition of these faces in the crowd;
Petals on a wet, black bough.

EZRA POUND WAS BORN IN HAILEY, IDAHO IN 1885. IN 1924, HE MOVED TO ITALY AND BECAME INVOLVED IN FASCIST POLITICS. UPON RETURNING TO THE UNITED STATES, HE WAS ARRESTED ON CHARGES OF TREASON AND EVENTUALLY COMMITTED TO A HOSPITAL. DURING HIS CONFINEMENT, THE LIBRARY OF CONGRESS AWARDED HIM THE BOLLINGEN PRIZE FOR THE *PISAN CANTOS* (1948). POUND DIED IN 1972.

Ezra Pound, poet and admired editor, whose unfortunate political beliefs often overshadow his place in the pantheon of the Modern poets, wrote some great poems, helped T. S. Eliot shape The Waste Land, and did some dazzling translations of Chinese poetry into English. It is perhaps the latter of those three achievements that led to this poem and others in his canon. By establishing the location of the poem in the title, IN A STATION AT THE METRO, the vivid image that follows completes the poem and one is transported to that literary station of the mind's eye where the "apparition of these faces in the crowd" instantly become "petals on a wet black bough." The poem is apprehended and its imagery is established so quickly that it is over faster than a train passing in the Paris Metro.

Whoosh: a poem.

-Michael O'Keefe

Passengers

DENIS JOHNSON

The world will burst like an intestine in the sun,
the dark turn to granite and the granite to a name,
but there will always be somebody riding the bus
through these intersections strewn with broken glass
among speechless women beating their little ones,
always a slow alphabet of rain
speaking of drifting and perishing to the air,
always these definite jails of light in the sky
at the wedding of this clarity and this storm
and a women's turning—her languid flight of hair
traveling through frame after frame of memory
where the past turns, its face sparking like emery,
to open its grace and incredible harm
over my life, and I will never die.

DENIS JOHNSON WAS BORN IN MUNICH, GERMANY IN 1949. AFTER STRUGGLING WITH ALCOHOLISM AND OTHER ADDICTIONS, HE WROTE *JESUS' SON*, A VOLUME OF STORIES WHICH WAS PUBLISHED TO MUCH ACCLAIM. JOHNSON'S HONORS INCLUDE A 1993 LANNAN FELLOWSHIP IN FICTION AND THE AGA KHAN PRIZE FOR FICTION FROM THE *PARIS REVIEW*. HE LIVES AND TEACHES IN SAN MARCOS, TEXAS.

Denis Johnson's book of poems, Incognito Lounge, served as an inspiration for many poets. The brilliance of PASSENGERS is the seamless transition Johnson makes between the minutiae of his dark worldview to a broader transcendence of that world, which trumps any darkness that precedes it. Part Zen Master, part tortured junkie, his narrator threads a needle with insight, mainlines it, and takes a

compelling trip where suffering lingers on the edge of every ecstasy. "The world" bursts "like an intestine in the sun." "The dark turn to granite," that is to say, darkness becomes solid. Meanwhile, "there will always be somebody riding the bus/through these intersections strewn with broken glass." An image of the infinite followed by one that grounds itself in the everyday sadness of bus rides populated by women hitting their kids. Yes, the world ends, daily, but still, it goes on. Later in the poem, at a "wedding of this clarity and this storm," a woman turns. "Her languid flight of hair/traveling through frame after frame of memory/where the past turns, its face sparking like emery," (notice that slant rhyme), "to open its grace and incredible harm/over my life." But that's not the end. In the end Johnson, his narrator, and all of us "will never die," because to read Denis Johnson is to get hooked on the dark side of transcendence. That lasts more than a lifetime

-Michael O'Keefe

MARY-LOUISE PARKER

To You

KENNETH KOCH

I love you as a sheriff searches for a walnut
That will solve a murder case unsolved for years
Because the murderer left it in the snow beside a window
Through which he saw her head, connecting with
Her shoulders by a neck, and laid a red
Roof in her heart. For this we live a thousand years;
For this we love, and we live because we love, we are not
Inside a bottle, thank goodness! I love you as a
Kid searches for a goat; I am crazier than shirttails
In the wind, when you're near, a wind that blows from
The big blue sea, so shiny so deep and so unlike us;
I think I am bicycling across an Africa of green and white fields
Always, to be near you, even in my heart
When I'm awake, which swims, and also I believe that you
Are trustworthy as the sidewalk which leads me to
The place where I again think of you, a new
Harmony of thoughts! I love you as the sunlight leads the prow
Of a ship which sails
From Hartford to Miami, and I love you
Best at dawn, when even before I am awake the sun
Receives me in the questions which you always pose.

KENNETH KOCH WAS BORN IN CINCINNATI, OHIO IN 1925. HIS COLLECTIONS OF POETRY INCLUDE *NEW ADDRESSES* (2000), A FINALIST FOR THE NATIONAL BOOK AWARD, AMONG MANY OTHERS. HE RECEIVED AWARDS FROM THE AMERICAN ACADEMY OF ARTS AND LETTERS AND THE FULBRIGHT, GUGGENHEIM, AND INGRAM-MERRILL FOUNDATIONS. KOCH DIED FROM LEUKEMIA IN 2002.

Keeping Things Whole

MARK STRAND

In a field
I am the absence
of field.
This is
always the case.
Wherever I am
I am what is missing.

When I walk
I part the air
and always
the air moves in
to fill the spaces
where my body's been.

We all have reasons
for moving.
I move
to keep things whole.

MARK STRAND IS THE AUTHOR OF NUMEROUS COLLECTIONS OF POETRY, INCLUDING *BLIZZARD OF ONE* (1998), A PULITZER PRIZE WINNER. HIS HONORS INCLUDE THREE GRANTS FROM THE NATIONAL ENDOWMENT FOR THE ARTS AND A ROCKEFELLER FOUNDATION AWARD. HE HAS SERVED AS POET LAUREATE OF THE UNITED STATES AND CURRENTLY TEACHES ENGLISH AND COMPARATIVE LITERATURE AT COLUMBIA UNIVERSITY IN NEW YORK.

TO YOU is one of the first poems i fell in love with. my heart rarely stops when i meet another person, but a poem or two has knocked me on my back upon first read and this is definitely one. i love the giddiness of it, the way it sort of trips over itself with such unabashed enthusiasm and sweetness. it's told so unselfconsciously, but with enormous skill and wit. i almost feel as though its being told as one big explosion after someone held their breath (or their pen) for longer than they could bear. i keep it taped to my wall.

KEEPING THINGS WHOLE is, i feel, one of the more profound poems in the english language. somewhat like elizabeth bishop's "in the waiting room" in that it touches on the nature of our mortal existence and how it can hit us from nowhere and rock us to our core. mark told me that this poem came to him in the middle of a card game with donald justice; he excused himself and left the table to write it out in a matter of minutes, never to rewrite it. aside from being haunting and just another of his great poems, i feel this one is important on a different level. he articulates something with a poetic image that never occurred to me before, with a kind of emotion that seems open to interpretation. it's a generous, honest poem.

-Mary-Louise Parker

KYRA
SEDGWICK

The Kitchen

JOCELYN WRIGHT

The pressure...
The pressure is on to be
tall
thin
and blonde
To be worked out enough to be firm
But not muscle-y enough to be masculinely strong
To be demure and deferential when you tell a man he is wrong
To be coiffed and well groomed at all hours of the day
Women are still cooking in the pressure pot
Cause little girls are being raised to be hot hot hot

THE KITCHEN, written by my dear friend Jocelyn, is a brilliant commentary
on the difficulties of being a woman trying to live up to society's expectations.
I love the use of the kitchen and the pressure pot as a metaphor.

-Kyra Sedgwick

PAUL
SIMON

The Long Boat
STANLEY KUNITZ

When his boat snapped loose
from its moorings, under
the screaking of the gulls,
he tried at first to wave
to his dear ones on shore,
but in the rolling fog
they had already lost their faces.
Too tired even to choose
between jumping and calling,
somehow he felt absolved and free
of his burdens, those mottoes
stamped on his name-tag:
conscience, ambition, and all
that caring.
He was content to lie down
with the family ghosts
in the slop of his cradle,
buffeted by the storm,
endlessly drifting.
Peace! Peace!
To be rocked by the Infinite!
As if it didn't matter
which way was home;
as if he didn't know
he loved the earth so much
he wanted to stay forever.

STANLEY KUNITZ WAS BORN IN WORCESTER, MASSACHUSETTS, IN 1905. KUNITZ PUBLISHED HIS FIRST BOOK OF POETRY, *INTELLECTUAL THINGS*, IN 1930. DEEPLY COMMITTED TO FOSTERING COMMUNITY AMONG ARTISTS, HE WAS A FOUNDER OF THE FINE ARTS WORK CENTER IN PROVINCETOWN, MASSACHUSETTS, AND POETS HOUSE IN NEW YORK CITY. KUNITZ RECEIVED MANY HONORS FOR HIS POETRY WORKS, INCLUDING A NATIONAL BOOK AWARD, THE LENORE MARSHALL POETRY PRIZE AND THE PULITZER PRIZE. HE ALSO SERVED AS UNITED STATES POET LAUREATE IN 2000. KUNITZ DIED AT THE AGE OF 100 IN 2006.

STEWART STERN

The Pasture

ROBERT FROST

I'm going out to clean the pasture spring;
I'll only stop to rake the leaves away
(And wait to watch the clear water, I may):
I sha'nt be gone long.—You come too.

I'm going out to fetch the little calf
That's standing by the mother. It's too young,
It totters when she licks it with her tongue.
I sha'nt be gone long.—You come too.

ROBERT FROST WAS BORN IN SAN FRANCISCO IN 1874. HIS FIRST PROFESSIONAL POEM, *MY BUTTERFLY*, WAS PUBLISHED IN 1894 IN THE NEW YORK NEWSPAPER, *THE INDEPENDENT*. BY THE 1920S, HE HAD WON FOUR PULITZER PRIZES AND PUBLISHED POETRY BOOKS ENTITLED *NEW HAMPSHIRE* (1923), *A FURTHER RANGE* (1936), *STEEPLE BUSH* (1947), AND *IN THE CLEARING* (1962) TO MUCH ACCLAIM. FROST DIED IN 1963.

Forgive, O Lord...

ROBERT FROST

Forgive, O Lord, my little jokes on Thee
and I'll forgive Thy great big one on me.

THE PASTURE was taught to me by my favorite teacher, Miss Angie Lois Purinton of Augusta, Maine, at the Ethical Culture School when I was 11. Miss Purinton, who was very imposing, wore fierce glasses and a hearing aid and believed that every school day should begin with a poem, preferably by Frost, and we each had our day to recite one. She had eyes that picked you out the way searchlights catch convicts halfway down a prison wall, a look that made you tremble, shook your soul and polished it till it came up to her standards and those grew into your own. She wouldn't lead her pupils to lunch until some boy remembered to bring her smock from the cloakroom and two others leaped to open the door. And after lunch she'd sit on the classroom floor and play Jacks with us and usually won. I went to visit her in Augusta when she was too old to recognize me, but she knew me, and she gave me a tile off her dining room wall that she had made in Miss Gillette's art class with the Japanese word for Truth on it in bas-relief. It keeps me honest when I write. She knew I loved cows with calves that tottered, that, I too, cleaned pasture springs, and that Frost's wonderful invitation, "You come too", would be an emblem of my life as it was hers. Miss Purinton had been gone for many years when I married, but saying the poem to my bride at our wedding was how I invited her to the altar, and part of me was proud that Miss Purinton would know that I remembered it.

FORGIVE, O LORD... is always there near my bed like a fireman's boots, ready to leap into quickly when the alarm goes off...

-Stewart Stern

DAVID
STRATHAIRN

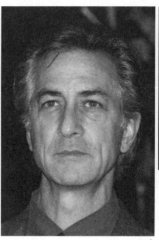

Eurydice's Hairpin. Cassandra's Curse

ADAM LeFEVRE

These are the names of wildflowers
that come out just at night,
in the remotest woods,
during no moon.

You can't hunt them with a flashlight or a match.
They'll get wind of any glimmer and close up
and slip back into the earth.

Even the invisible light of your own eyes
will frighten them.

You have to go on hands and knees, eyes closed
groping delicately with your fingers.

It's painful.

When you come home
at sunrise, hands bloody, forehead bumped
and blue, the knees of your pants torn through,
your loved ones call you "crazy idiot."

But never mind.
They are not your loved ones.
These flowers are.

And when you find them,
when you hold them in your hands,
you get one wish, beginning
I don't want

ADAM LEFEVRE IS AN ACTOR WHO HAS MOST RECENTLY APPEARED IN *HITCH* AND *MISS CONGENIALITY 2*. BORN IN NEW YORK IN 1950, LEFEVRE HAS TWO GRADUATE DEGREES FROM THE UNIVERSITY OF IOWA, FOR THE PLAYWRIGHTS' WORKSHOP, AND THE WRITERS' WORKSHOP.

I return to Adam's poem because, for me, it captures the heart of the journey towards discovery in rigorous personal exploration, no matter what discipline. And the ambiguity of "I don't want" has true compassion and grace.
-David Strathairn

HOLLAND TAYLOR

TRACKS 25,26

Dulce et Decorum Est

WILFRED OWEN

Bent double, like old beggars under sacks,
Knock-kneed, coughing like hags, we cursed through sludge,
Till on the haunting flares we turned our backs
And towards our distant rest began to trudge.
Men marched asleep. Many had lost their boots
But limped on, blood-shod. All went lame; all blind;
Drunk with fatigue; deaf even to the hoots
Of tired, outstripped Five-Nines that dropped behind.

Gas! Gas! Quick, boys!—An ecstasy of fumbling,
Fitting the clumsy helmets just in time;
But someone still was yelling out and stumbling
And flound'ring like a man in fire or lime…
Dim, through the misty panes and thick green light,
As under a green sea, I saw him drowning.

In all my dreams, before my helpless sight,
He plunges at me, guttering, choking, drowning.

If in some smothering dreams you too could pace
Behind the wagon that we flung him in,
And watch the white eyes writhing in his face,
His hanging face, like a devil's sick of sin;
If you could hear, at every jolt, the blood
Come gargling from the froth-corrupted lungs,
Obscene as cancer, bitter as the cud
Of vile, incurable sores on innocent tongues,—
My friend, you would not tell with such high zest
To children ardent for some desperate glory,
The old Lie: *Dulce et decorum est*
Pro patria mori.

WILFRED OWEN WAS BORN IN 1893 IN SHROPSHIRE, ENGLAND. IN 1915, HE ENLISTED IN THE ARTISTS' RIFLES GROUP AND WAS WOUNDED IN COMBAT IN 1917. WHILE RECOVERING OWEN WROTE MANY POEMS INCLUDING "ANTHEM FOR DOOMED YOUTH" AND "DULCE ET DECORUM EST." OWEN REJOINED HIS REGIMENT IN 1918 AND WAS AWARDED THE MILITARY CROSS. HE DIED THAT SAME YEAR WHILE SERVING.

My love is multi-lateral

JEAN PEDRICK

My love is multi-lateral, and faintly Lady Chatteral
Filled with dog and catteral
Always flying blind
For I love an honest body with a love that's somewhat shoddy
But my other self, less naughty,
Loves an honest mind.

JEAN PEDRICK WAS BORN IN 1922 IN SALEM, MASSACHUSETTS. SHE CO-FOUNDED THE ALICE JAMES POETRY COOPERATIVE, WHICH LATER BECAME KNOWN AS ALICE JAMES BOOKS. IN 1993, PEDRICK WON THE BRUCE ROSSLEY LITERARY AWARD, WHICH RECOGNIZES THE UNDER-RECOGNIZED LITERARY VOICES OF THE CITY OF BOSTON, AND IN 2003, SHE PUBLISHED *CATGUT*, HER LAST FULL-LENGTH COLLECTION OF POETRY. PEDRICK DIED IN 2006 FOLLOWING A STROKE.

David Dukes and I met during the shooting of an ill-fated American TV series, loosely based on Upstairs/Downstairs, called Beacon Hill. It took place in Boston during the first World War, and David played the scion of the aristocratic family, a dashing young officer who had lost an arm in

battle and who was gorgeous and tortured. I felt vaguely fluttery whenever he was around, as I recall. Some years later he did a play at the Public, in which he was a dashing officer in the Civil War. I continued to be a little dreamy about him. I think it was then that I lent him my copy of Wilfred Owen's book of poetry, which had an impossibly beautiful and tragic photograph in grainy black and white on the cover. I remember him doing one of the poems, I think from memory, and that was, I guess, one of the most celebrated, DULCE ET DECORUM EST. Over the years, he kept saying, "Damn, I must return that book to you!" but I was content to leave it with him, as it was a thread of my occasional romantic musings in his direction. Years later, I went to see him in Stoppard's Travesties, and on the wave of excitement I always felt watching him act I resolved to make a move! I don't remember (mercifully) what form my "pass" took in his dressing room after the show, but he charmingly told me he was just then seeing this great girl, who of course turned out to be the poet Carol Muske, and the rest was history! I then gracefully sent him this poem by my acquaintance Jean Pedrick, now gone to her reward. I have to share it from memory, as I can find it nowhere in print. Many years later, he returned the Wilfred Owen when I was having dinner with him and Carol one balmy summer evening at their airy and delightful family home in Hancock Park. We were friends.

-Holland Taylor

LILI TAYLOR

TRACKS 27,28

The Road Not Taken

ROBERT FROST

Two roads diverged in a yellow wood,
And sorry I could not travel both
And be one traveler, long I stood
And looked down one as far as I could
To where it bent in the undergrowth;

Then took the other, as just as fair,
And having perhaps the better claim,
Because it was grassy and wanted wear;
Though as for that the passing there
Had worn them really about the same,

And both that morning equally lay
In leaves no step had trodden black.
Oh, I kept the first for another day!
Yet knowing how way leads on to way,
I doubted if I should ever come back

I shall be telling this with a sigh
Somewhere ages and ages hence:
Two roads diverged in a wood, and I—
I took the one less traveled by,
And that has made all the difference.

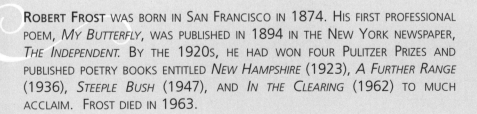

ROBERT FROST WAS BORN IN SAN FRANCISCO IN 1874. HIS FIRST PROFESSIONAL POEM, *MY BUTTERFLY*, WAS PUBLISHED IN 1894 IN THE NEW YORK NEWSPAPER, *THE INDEPENDENT*. BY THE 1920S, HE HAD WON FOUR PULITZER PRIZES AND PUBLISHED POETRY BOOKS ENTITLED *NEW HAMPSHIRE* (1923), *A FURTHER RANGE* (1936), *STEEPLE BUSH* (1947), AND *IN THE CLEARING* (1962) TO MUCH ACCLAIM. FROST DIED IN 1963.

Say Yes Quickly
RUMI
TRANSLATED BY COLEMAN BARKS

Forget your life.
Say *God is Great.* Get up.
You think you know
what time it is.
It's time to pray.
You've carved so many little figurines, too many.
Don't knock on any random door like a beggar.
Reach your long hands out
to another door, beyond where
you go on the street, the street
where everyone says, "How are you?"
and no one says How aren't you?

RUMI WAS A THIRTEENTH-CENTURY PERSIAN MUSLIM POET, JURIST AND THEOLOGIAN, BORN IN BALKH (PRESENT-DAY AFGHANISTAN). RUMI'S MAJOR WORK IS *MASNAVI-YE MANAVI* (SPIRITUAL COUPLETS), A SIX-VOLUME POEM REGARDED BY MANY SUFI MUSLIMS AS SECOND IN IMPORTANCE ONLY TO THE QUR'AN, ALONG WITH THE DIVAN-I KEBIR OR *DIWAN-E SHAMS-E TABRIZ-I* (THE WORKS OF SHAMS OF TABRIZ), COMPRISING SOME 40,000 VERSES.

i have been doing this a while now. i say with a sigh but yesterday said
with a smile and tomorrow who knows.
poems are a form of prayer for me.
i am in the woods. it is morning. it is autumn.
i can hear. sort of.
i will go this way.

and i will stand by it because in the woods in the autumn with the sun i
am aware of something bigger than me.
and years later i don't have to understand or even like it.
but it's what i did and it's me. and it's more than me.

-Lili Taylor

STANLEY
TUCCI

Children, It's Spring

MARY OLIVER

And this is lady
whom everyone loves,
Ms. Violet
in her purple gown

or, on special occasions,
a dress the color
of sunlight. She sits
in the mossy weeds and waits

to be noticed.
She loves dampness.
She loves attention.
She loves especially

to be picked by careful fingers,
young fingers, entranced
by what has happened
to the world.

We, the older ones,
call it Spring,
and we have been through it
many times.

But there is still nothing
like the children bringing home
such happiness
in their small hands.

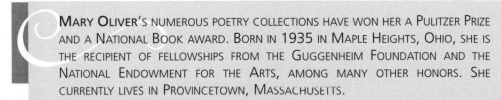

MARY OLIVER'S NUMEROUS POETRY COLLECTIONS HAVE WON HER A PULITZER PRIZE AND A NATIONAL BOOK AWARD. BORN IN 1935 IN MAPLE HEIGHTS, OHIO, SHE IS THE RECIPIENT OF FELLOWSHIPS FROM THE GUGGENHEIM FOUNDATION AND THE NATIONAL ENDOWMENT FOR THE ARTS, AMONG MANY OTHER HONORS. SHE CURRENTLY LIVES IN PROVINCETOWN, MASSACHUSETTS.

Alone

ANONYMOUS

Alone.

This is a poem that I read to the class when I was in seventh grade. We all were reading poems of our choosing and I read one, (I don't know what it was), and then I said I'd like to read another. It was, from my recollection, an anonymous American Indian poem. The authorship may be vague in my mind but the poem is most distinct. It goes as follows:

Alone.

It was to me the perfect poem. It was at once profound and funny, not unlike...life.

-Stanley Tucci

TAIKA WAITITI

The Tyger

WILLIAM BLAKE

TYGER, Tyger, burning bright
In the forests of the night,
What immortal hand or eye
Could frame thy fearful symmetry?

In what distant deeps or skies
Burnt the fire of thine eyes?
On what wings dare he aspire?
What the hand dare seize the fire?

And what shoulder and what art
Could twist the sinews of thy heart?
And when thy heart began to beat,
What dread hand? and what dread feet?

What the hammer? what the chain?
In what furnace was thy brain?
What the anvil? What dread grasp
Dare its deadly terrors clasp?

When the stars threw down their spears,
And water'd heaven with their tears,
Did He smile His work to see?
Did He who made the lamb make thee?

Tyger, Tyger, burning bright
In the forests of the night,
What immortal hand or eye
Dare frame thy fearful symmetry?

WILLIAM BLAKE, BORN IN LONDON IN 1757, WAS A POET AND ARTIST. THOUGH SPENDING MOST OF HIS LIFE WORKING ON ILLUSTRATIONS, ENGRAVING, AND WATERCOLORS, BLAKE BEGAN WRITING POETRY AT AGE 12. HIS FIRST PUBLISHED WORK, *POETICAL SKETCHES*, CAME OUT IN 1783. BLAKE SPENT HIS FINAL YEARS IN POVERTY, WORKING ON ILLUSTRATIONS UNTIL HIS DEATH IN 1827.

My mother, an English teacher, made me study this poem one Saturday as a child. At the time I was frustrated by its many meanings and questions within questions but later came to appreciate its layered simplicity. I think it's a great skill to ask one question which makes people ask four more in return. Or is it? This poem needs to be read very loudly during the courtroom scene in Kramer vs. Kramer.

-Taika Waititi

Night on the Island

PABLO NERUDA
TRANSLATED BY DONALD D. WALSH

All night I have slept with you
next to the sea, on the island.
Wild and sweet you were between pleasure and sleep,
between fire and water.

Perhaps very late
our dreams joined
at the top or at the bottom,
up above like branches moved by a common wind,
down below like red roots that touch.

Perhaps your dream
drifted from mine
and through the dark sea
was seeking me
as before,
when you did not yet exist,
when without sighting you
I sailed by your side,
and your eyes sought
what now—
bread, wine, love, and anger—
I heap upon you
because you are the cup
that was waiting for the gifts of my life.

I have slept with you
all night long while
the dark earth spins
with the living and the dead,
and on waking suddenly
in the midst of the shadow
my arm encircled your waist.

Neither night nor sleep
could separate us.

I have slept with you
and on waking, your mouth,
come from your dream,
gave me the taste of earth,
of sea water, of seaweed,
of the depths of your life,
and I received your kiss
moistened by the dawn
as if it came to me
from the sea that surrounds us.

PABLO NERUDA WAS BORN IN SOUTHERN CHILE IN 1904. IN 1923, HE SOLD ALL OF HIS POSSESSIONS TO FINANCE THE PUBLICATION OF HIS FIRST BOOK, *CREPUSCULARIO* (TWILIGHT). NERUDA RECEIVED NUMEROUS AWARDS, INCLUDING THE INTERNATIONAL PEACE PRIZE, THE LENIN PEACE PRIZE, THE STALIN PEACE PRIZE, AND THE NOBEL PRIZE FOR LITERATURE. HE DIED OF LEUKEMIA IN 1973.

If everyone could speak truth like this I think the world would collapse upon itself. There would be chaos. That is why only a few of us get to be poets. This beautiful thing reminds me why I'm not one. It holds many images and feelings which I have felt, seen or imagined but never known how to put into words. Poets are our real mouths, they speak for us, expressing what we cannot. Its a big job with very little pay. I recommend reading this with a large priceless vase balanced on your head whilst standing in a circle of 200 screaming babies.

-Taika Waititi

GEORGE WENDT

⟨ TRACK 29

from *Hamlet, Act 3, Scene 2*

WILLIAM SHAKESPEARE

Speak the speech, I pray you, as I pronounce it to you, trippingly on the tongue.
But if you mouth it, as many of our players do—I had as lief the town-crier spoke
my lines. Nor do not saw the air too much with your hand, thus, but use all gently,
for in the very torrent tempest, and as I may say whirlwind of your passion, you
must acquire and beget a temperance that may give it smoothness. O, it offends me
to the soul to hear a robustious periwig-pated fellow tear a passion to tatters, to
very rags, to split the ears of the groundlings, who for the most part are capable of
nothing but inexplicable dumb shows and noise. I would have such a fellow
whipped for o'erdoing Termagant. It out-herods Herod. Pray you, avoid it.

Like all actors, Hamlet's speech speaks to me, "trippingly on the tongue."
-George Wendt

White Key (for David)

CAROL MUSKE-DUKES

The mountains shut their doors,
Once, twice, in the shadow of the jet
Turning east over the continent,

As it widens like the light on the bed
In the blue room where I last held you.
Out there, the palms in quilted barks

Line up, symmetrical as rain,
A red bird repeats its single question
At each descending step of sleep.

For too long I've been dreaming the dream
About prison, turning in circles on that cracked
Floor, trying to wake — as easily as I woke

This morning, the sun inching its proscenium
Of shadow forward to the glass doors I slid open
And walked through — blinded by one floating

Light-puzzle after another: stone Buddha,
Red petals, pool, you smiling, already awake.
In hours, the plane circles above the kingdom

Of realized wishes, my city, (since cities are
Owned by thought and thought is possessive).
Above the pale night clouds: one star, white key

In a white ignition. What do we deserve on this earth?
Not to be lied to by the mind, the body bent by that
Conscious wind into habits of the cage. To not

Hurt, to not betray, to not be prey of evil people,
Drink or pain. The last sculpture of clothes we
Left near the bed drifts in that wind. You are sure

Of yourself, friend, and I like that. The plane hovers
Over its perfectly-marked lines of entry—like thought
Flying parallel to revelation—dreaming of all the places

Along its body it could intersect with sudden light.
We wake up, if we are lucky, once in our lives.
The wheels touch earth, we lean up into love,

Not blind, more white on white, a key unseen
In a cylinder of entry, a handful of passengers
Taking quick ecstatic stock—beginning, one

By one, on a plane, to applaud.

CAROL MUSKE-DUKES IS A TEACHER AND THE AUTHOR OF SEVEN BOOKS OF POETRY AND THREE NOVELS. HER FIRST BOOK OF POEMS, *CAMOUFLAGE*, WAS PUBLISHED IN 1975. HER MOST RECENT VOLUME OF POETRY, *SPARROW* (2003), WAS A NATIONAL BOOK AWARD FINALIST. AMONG HER AWARDS ARE A 1981 GUGGENHEIM FELLOWSHIP AND SEVERAL PUSHCART PRIZES. SHE CURRENTLY LIVES IN LOS ANGELES AND WRITES A POETRY COLUMN FOR THE *LOS ANGELES TIMES*.

I was moved when I heard Carol read her poem WHITE KEY at David's funeral, not only because I loved and admired David (he and I and Stacy Keach were in the play Art together in London's West End), but because the poem reminded me of a familiar situation in my own life, flying back & forth across the country, to be with loved ones, to live one's life.
-George Wendt

DIANNE
WIEST

Black Rook in Rainy Weather

SYLVIA PLATH

On the stiff twig up there
Hunches a wet black rook
Arranging and rearranging its feathers in the rain.
I do not expect a miracle
Or an accident

To set the sight on fire
In my eye, nor seek
Any more in the desultory weather some design,
But let spotted leaves fall as they fall,
Without ceremony, or portent.

Although, I admit, I desire,
Occasionally, some backtalk
From the mute sky, I can't honestly complain:
A certain minor light may still
Lean incandescent

Out of kitchen table or chair
As if a celestial burning took
Possession of the most obtuse objects now and then –
Thus hallowing an interval
Otherwise inconsequent

By bestowing largess, honor,
One might say love. At any rate, I now walk
Wary (for it could happen
Even in this dull, ruinous landscape); skeptical
Yet politic; ignorant

Of whatever angel may choose to flare
Suddenly at my elbow. I only know that a rook
Ordering its black feathers can so shine
As to seize my senses, haul
My eyelids up, and grant

A brief respite from fear
Of total neutrality. With luck,
Trekking stubborn through this season
Of fatigue, I shall
Patch together a content

Of sorts. Miracles occur,
If you care to call those spasmodic
Tricks of radiance miracles. The wait's begun again,
The long wait for the angel,
For that rare, random descent.

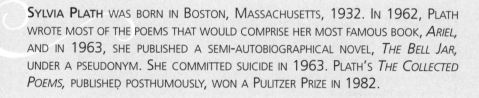

SYLVIA PLATH WAS BORN IN BOSTON, MASSACHUSETTS, 1932. IN 1962, PLATH WROTE MOST OF THE POEMS THAT WOULD COMPRISE HER MOST FAMOUS BOOK, *ARIEL*, AND IN 1963, SHE PUBLISHED A SEMI-AUTOBIOGRAPHICAL NOVEL, *THE BELL JAR*, UNDER A PSEUDONYM. SHE COMMITTED SUICIDE IN 1963. PLATH'S *THE COLLECTED POEMS*, PUBLISHED POSTHUMOUSLY, WON A PULITZER PRIZE IN 1982.

The River-Merchant's Wife: A Letter

EZRA POUND
TRANSLATED FROM THE ORIGINAL BY RIHAKU (LI T'AI PO)

While my hair was still cut straight across my forehead
I played about the front gate, pulling flowers.
You came by on bamboo stilts, playing horse,
You walked about my seat, playing with blue plums.
And we went on living in the village of Chōkan:
Two small people, without dislike or suspicion.

At fourteen I married My Lord you.
I never laughed, being bashful.
Lowering my head, I looked at the wall.
Called to, a thousand times, I never looked back.

At fifteen I stopped scowling,
I desired my dust to be mingled with yours
Forever and forever and forever.
Why should I climb the look out?

At sixteen you departed,
You went into far Ku-tō-en, by the river of swirling eddies,
And you have been gone five months.
The monkeys make sorrowful noise overhead.

You dragged your feet when you went out.
By the gate now, the moss is grown, the different mosses,
Too deep to clear them away!
The leaves fall early this autumn, in wind.
The paired butterflies are already yellow with August
Over the grass in the West garden;
They hurt me. I grow older.
If you are coming down through the narrows of the river Kiang,
Please let me know beforehand,
And I will come out to meet you
                    As far as Chó-fú-Sa.

EZRA POUND WAS BORN IN HAILEY, IDAHO IN 1885. IN 1924, HE MOVED TO ITALY AND BECAME INVOLVED IN FASCIST POLITICS. UPON RETURNING TO THE UNITED STATES, HE WAS ARRESTED ON CHARGES OF TREASON AND EVENTUALLY COMMITTED TO A HOSPITAL. DURING HIS CONFINEMENT, THE LIBRARY OF CONGRESS AWARDED HIM THE BOLLINGEN PRIZE FOR THE *PISAN CANTOS* (1948). POUND DIED IN 1972.

It's so difficult to say why you love a poem, because what you would say about the poem is there—in the poem! A poem's exquisite combination of words that say precisely what I've always felt but could never describe or tell anyone except within a mishmash of emotions astonishes me.
I am always relieved to read these two particular poems, to be able to say to myself: Yes—exactly like this! THE RIVER-MERCHANT'S WIFE : A LETTER was given to me by a boy, thirty-five years ago and BLACK ROOK IN RAINY WEATHER was given to me by Carol Muske-Dukes two years ago—for me to read at an Academy of American Poets gala.

These great poems are, like all poems, outside of time.
-Dianne Wiest

ALFRE WOODARD

Ego Tripping
(There May Be A Reason Why)

NIKKI GIOVANNI

I was born in the congo
I walked to the fertile crescent and built
  the sphinx
I designed a pyramid so tough that a star
  that only glows every one hundred years falls
  into the center giving divine perfect light
I am bad

I sat on the throne
  drinking nectar with allah
I got hot and sent an ice age to europe
  to cool my thirst
My oldest daughter is nefertiti
  the tears from my birth pains
  created the nile
I am a beautiful woman

I gazed on the forest and burned
  out the sahara desert
  with a packet of goat's meat
  and a change of clothes
I crossed it in two hours
I am a gazelle so swift
  so swift you can't catch me

  For a birthday present when he was three
I gave my son hannibal an elephant
  He gave me rome for mother's day
My strength flows ever on

My son noah built new/ark and
I stood proudly at the helm
  as we sailed on a soft summer day

I turned myself into myself and was
 jesus
 men intone my loving name
 All praises All praises
I am the one who would save

I sowed diamonds in my back yard
My bowels deliver uranium
 the filings from my fingernails are
 semi-precious jewels
 On a trip north
I caught a cold and blew
My nose giving oil to the arab world
I am so hip even my errors are correct
I sailed west to reach east and had to round off
 the earth as I went
 The hair from my head thinned and gold was laid
 across three continents

I am so perfect so divine so ethereal so surreal
I cannot be comprehended
   except by my permission

I mean...I...can fly
 like a bird in the sky...

NIKKI GIOVANNI RECEIVED THREE NAACP IMAGE AWARDS FOR LITERATURE IN 1998 AND THE LANGSTON HUGHES AWARD FOR DISTINGUISHED CONTRIBUTIONS TO ARTS AND LETTERS IN 1996. IN 2007, SHE BECAME THE FIRST POET AWARDED THE CARL SANDBURG LITERARY AWARD FROM THE CHICAGO PUBLIC LIBRARY FOUNDATION. SEVERAL MAGAZINES HAVE NAMED GIOVANNI WOMAN OF THE YEAR, INCLUDING ESSENCE AND LADIES HOME JOURNAL. SHE IS CURRENTLY A PROFESSOR AT VIRGINIA TECH UNIVERSITY.

When a Beggar Beholds You

ANONYMOUS
TRANSLATED BY GERTRUDE C. JOERISSEN

When the breeze inflates your two robes of silk
you look like a Goddess enveloped in clouds.

When you pass, the flowers of the mulberry tree
drink in your perfume. When you carry the lilacs
that you have gathered, they tremble with joy.

Bands of gold encircle your ankles, stones of blue
gleam in your girdle. A bird of jade has made its
nest in your hair. The roses of your cheeks mirror
themselves in the great pearls of your collar.

When you look at me I see the river Yuen flowing.
When you speak to me I hear the music of the
wind among the pines of my own country.

When a horseman meets you at dusk he thinks
it is already dawn, and brutally he brings his
horse to a standstill

....When a beggar beholds you, he forgets his hunger.

If you've grown up expendable in America as a knobby-kneed little black girl with your short nappy plaits flying in every direction, discovering Nikki Giovanni's EGO TRIPPING at seventeen is like drinking sparkling spring water for the first time. It cooled a thirst I didn't know I had.

In the middle of a dominant culture of leggy blondes with upturned noses and creamy unmarked skin, Sister Nikki held up the mirror of history so that I could see my true reflection. I stood all the way up in that grounding, and in beauty I rocked my wide hips and strode all across the city. It still keeps me "walkin' it out"!

WHEN A BEGGAR BEHOLDS YOU. This poem is hot. The beholder is consumed, captivated by the vision. It's been twenty-six years, and I want my husband to see me that way still. Others too, but I go home with him.

-Alfre Woodard

David Coleman Dukes, Carol Muske-Dukes, and John Lithgow

In memory of David Coleman Dukes, whose remarkable presence and participation as an actor, and appreciator of poetry, helped trigger the genesis of this book.

On David Dukes

I first heard the name David Dukes in 1971, when I learned who had been cast as the young romantic lead in a Broadway production of Moliere's SCHOOL FOR WIVES. I took a particular interest since I had auditioned for the role myself (one of my very first New York auditions) and I thought I had nailed it. "David Who?!" I asked, incredulously. Later I saw him in the play, and of course he was just wonderful. I'm no different from most actors: I generally don't much like to admit that someone else has acted a role better than I ever could. But in this case, it was true.

It was the first of many times I saw David onstage and on film, and I never felt the slightest tinge of actor's envy or injustice. He seemed to simply belong in every part he played. This was even true, perhaps especially so, when he was called upon to replace John Wood and Ian McKellan in their virtuosic roles in TRAVESTIES and AMADEUS, respectively. No one missed these estimable Englishmen when David took over. He was just as authoritative, just as brilliant.

But there was more to David the actor than his power onstage. He loved the process of the theatre, its company ethos, and its workmanlike, generous spirit. He would approach a small role in a radio play with the same verve and commitment as a starring role on Broadway. As a result, everyone loved to work with him.
Then there was David the husband, David the father, David the friend. Each of us felt lucky in our particular relationship with this man. The consummate actor shed all artifice when he was with us. He was a warm, lively, sardonic friend. He was a devoted and doting father. He admired his wife Carol as deeply as he loved her, and always seemed surprised and grateful that he'd had the incredible good fortune to find her.

Because David died so suddenly, at such a young age, and because the tragedy hit all of us so hard, we have tended to reflexively speak of him in terms of his death. No more of that! Here's to an actor who flat out loved to act. Here's to a loving, passionate man, vitally important to everyone who knew him. Here's to a full, joyous career and to a life well lived. Here's to David Dukes.

—JOHN LITHGOW, SEPTEMBER, 2007

The Machine

CAROL MUSKE-DUKES

Night after night when he was young,
he told me he dreamed the same dream.
It was not a simple dream, the machine.

At first it half-coalesced as a drill press
or lathe, a thing that controlled the direction
of force to alter shape. Parts turned: ratchets

gears, bearings. The machine in his troubled sleep
was a series of perfectable gestures in the spirit of
the cam-shaft: a projection on a rotating part

shaped to engender motion—but was not erotic exactly.
The machine was the point at which the lever was placed
to get purchase, the fulcrum, the means by which influence

is brought to bear, the chime of iron against iron in a holding rack,
power against resistance. What was its purpose as he perfected
it each night? Not to assemble or sort or tattoo patterns on metal.

It shimmered, a thousand lit pins, a system—a series of moving
parts that would never still, synchronous. What would it
replace? The erratic—manufactured as a strap—a father lashing

a son into a place of dark stasis. He stood up to audition and he had
the words at last, he'd gotten his mind round the mechanism, the facets,
the repetitive force of illusion, the jeweled speeches kept in memory

as he hammered the boards of the stage, hauled flats, swung one-handed
from the flies to set lights. Sometimes a person wakes up, sees he's meant
for another life—the snap-clasp of the theater trunk, the high-voltage moving spot—

commoner, lord, poet—the armored breastplate. Sometimes he looks in
the mirror and sees no self but the invention, fathomable, fashioned—
the shapes of Art, all makeable—as in the machine, his machine,
the machine that made him.

ABOUT DAVID COLEMAN DUKES

David Coleman Dukes (1945-2000) grew up in Marin County, California, and trained at the American Conservatory Theater. He appeared in over 24 movies, including *A Little Romance*, *First Deadly Sin*, *Without a Trace*, and *Gods and Monsters*. His extensive work in theater, for which he received Tony and Drama Desk nominations, began in his twenties, and included starring roles in the Broadway productions of *Amadeus*, *M. Butterfly*, *Bent*, *Someone to Watch Over Me*, and *Broken Glass*. His many TV and HBO appearances included *All in the Family*, *The Winds of War* and *War and Remembrance*, *Beacon Hill*, and the *Josephine Baker Story*, for which he received an Emmy nomination, as well as leading ongoing roles in *Sisters* and *Dawson's Creek*. He recorded over 50 books on tape, including Philip Roth's *Sabbath Theater*.

The David Coleman Dukes Memorial Theatre Scholarship Fund at the University of Southern California honors the late actor David Coleman Dukes and is presented to a senior B.A. or B.F.A. acting student who shows exemplary dedication to the craft of acting.

ABOUT THE CONTRIBUTORS

Adam Arkin was born in Brooklyn, New York. Currently, in the NBC drama *Life*, he has also appeared in several television series including *Law and Order*, *Frasier*, *Chicago Hope* and *Boston Legal*. His many recent film appearances include *Hitch* (2005) and *Halloween: H20* (1998). Arkin is also an award-winning Broadway and off-Broadway performer, last seen in "Brooklyn Boy" by playwright Donald Margulies.

Alan Arkin was born in New York City and moved to Los Angeles at age 11. He is best known for his starring roles in films such as *Catch-22*, *The In-Laws*, and *Little Miss Sunshine*, for which he won an Academy Award for Best Supporting Actor. He also won a Tony Award for his Broadway performance in *Enter Laughing*.

Jon Robin Baitz is a screenwriter and producer. He is the creator and executive producer of the ABC drama *Brothers and Sisters* and has also written for *The West Wing*. He has received a Guggenheim Fellowship, a Drama Desk Award and was a Pulitzer Prize finalist for *A Fair County*, which he authored.

Bob Balaban most recently directed and produced *Bernard and Doris*, starring Susan Sarandon and Ralph Fiennes. Balaban has appeared in over fifty movies, including *Midnight Cowboy*, *Close Encounters of the Third Kind*, *Best in Show*, *Gosford Park*, which he also produced and for which he won Academy and SAG awards and, most recently *The Lady in the Water* and *Capote*. He is also the author of the best-selling children's book series, "McGrowl."

Ken Brecher is the Executive Director of the Sundance Institute. He previously served as President of the William Penn Foundation and Director of the Boston Children's Museum. An anthropologist by training, Brecher is the recipient of numerous awards, including a Ford Foundation Fellowship for his study of Amazonian tribesmen in Brazil. His memoir, *Too Sad to Sing, a Memoir with Postcards*, was published by Harcourt in 1988. His installation, "The Little Room of Epiphanies," was at the Santa Monica Museum of Art in 2006.

Steve Buscemi is an actor and director born in Brooklyn, New York. He is perhaps best known for his roles in the movies *Reservoir Dogs*, *The Big Lebowski*, and *Fargo*, as well as *28 Days* and *Armageddon*. In 2004, he joined the cast of popular television series *The Sopranos* and also directed third and sixth season episodes. Buscemi is an associate member of the experimental theater company, The Wooster

Group. He will soon be seen in the movies *We're The Millers*, *Igor*, and *Coming Back*. He made his movie directorial debut with *Trees Lounge*, and recently directed *Animal Factory* and *Lonesome Jim*.

Billy Collins is the author of seven books of poetry, his latest being *The Trouble With Poetry and Other Poems* (Random House, 2005). He served as United States poet laureate from 2001 to 2003 and is a Distinguished Professor of English at Lehman College (City University of New York).

Brian Cox is an award-winning actor who has starred in more than 50 feature films, most recently *Running with Scissors* and *The Bourne Supremacy*. He has also authored two non-fiction books, *The Lear Diaries* and *Salem to Moscow: An Actor's Odyssey;* and in 2007 the UK Film Council named him one of the Top 10 powerful British film stars in Hollywood today.

Peter Coyote is a writer and an actor. He has appeared in more than 70 films, including *E.T.*, *Jagged Edge*, and *Die Coughing* and does extensive voice-over work, for which he has won an Emmy. His 1998 memoir, *Sleeping Where I Fall*, includes the Pushcart Prize-winning story, "Carla's Story," and is based on his experiences as part of the counter-culture community in the '60s and '70s.

Eve Ensler is the award-winning author of the play *The Vagina Monologues*. She also executive-produced *What I Want My Words To Do To You*, a documentary which earned the Freedom Of Expression Award at the 2003 Sundance Film Festival. Ensler has received many honors including the Guggenheim Fellowship Award in Playwriting.

Carrie Fisher is a best-selling author, screenwriter, and actress. She has appeared in such films as *When Harry Met Sally* and *Austin Powers: International Man of Mystery*. She made her film debut in *Shampoo* (1975) and went on to play Princess Leia in George Lucas' *Star Wars* trilogy. Her first novel, *Postcards From the Edge* (1987) was adapted for the screen. She continues to publish novels as well as appear in films and television.

Michael Fitzgerald has been producing films for over 25 years, including such movies as *Wise Blood*, *Under the Volcano*, *The Pledge*, and *The Three Burials of Melquiades Estrada*. He writes that he is "still alive with one wife, three children, ten films, ten thousand bottles of wine, two hundred and fifty thousand cigarettes, 1.8 billion heartbeats to answer for."

Jane Fonda is an actress, writer, and political activist who has won two Academy Awards for *Klute* (1971) and *Coming Home* (1978). She most recently appeared in *Georgia Rule* (2007). Fonda is an activist for many causes, including opposition to the Iraq War and support of V-Day, a movement to stop violence against women, inspired by "The Vagina Monologues."

Rodrigo Garcia is a Colombian-born film and television director. His most recent project is the 2008 thriller film *Passengers* starring Anne Hathaway. Garcia has received many honors for his work, including an Un Certain Regard Award for the film *Things You Can Tell Just by Looking at Her* (2000), which he wrote and directed.

Kathleen Glynn is the Emmy Award-winning producer of *TV Nation*, co-producer of *Canadian Bacon*, and producer of *The Big One*. She also worked with Michael Moore, as co-producer of *Roger and Me*, and producer of *Bowling for Columbine* (2002), *Fahrenheit 9/11* (2004), and *Sicko* (2007). Together they have also published a book, *Adventures in a TV Nation* (1998).

Paul Guilfoyle is well known for his role as Captain Jim Brass in the forensic drama series *CSI: Crime Scene Investigation* and has appeared in more than 70 films including *Mrs. Doubtfire, L.A. Confidential, Hoffa, Primary Colors, Quiz Show, Air Force One,* and most recently, HBO Film's *Live From Baghdad*. He has also appeared in Broadway productions of "Richard III" and "Those the River Keeps."

Daryl Hannah was born and raised in Chicago, Illinois. She has starred in acclaimed films such as *Splash* (1984), *Blade Runner, The Big Empty, Grumpy Old Men,* and, most recently *Kill Bill Volumes 1* and *2*. In 1994, she won the Jury Award from the Berlin International Film Festival for *The Last Supper*, which she wrote, directed, and produced. Hannah is also an activist for environmental and sexual slavery issues.

Philip Seymour Hoffman is currently appearing in Mike Nichols' *Charlie Wilson's War* and recently completed the independent feature *The Savages* with Laura Linney as well as Sidney Lumet's *Before the Devil Knows You're Dead*. He last appeared in *Mission: Impossible 3* and earned the Best Actor Academy Award in 2006 for his performance in *Capote*, which he executive produced through his film company, Cooper's Town Productions. Other acting credits: *Empire Falls* (HBO), *Cold Mountain, Owning Mahowny, Punch-Drunk Love, 25th Hour, Love Liza, Almost Famous, State and Main, Magnolia, The Talented Mr. Ripley, Boogie Nights, Happiness,* and *The Big Lebowski*. Hoffman is the Co-Artistic Director of LAByrinth Theater

Company. Stage credits (acting): *Long Day's Journey Into Night*; *The Seagull*; *True West*; *Defying Gravity*; and *The Merchant of Venice*. Directing credits: *The Glory of Living* at MCC Theater; and for LAByrinth, *In Arabia We'd All Be Kings*; *Jesus Hopped The 'A' Train* (Off-Broadway and London's West End); *Our Lady of 121st Street* (Union Square Theater); and *The Last Days of Judas Iscariot* (The Public Theater), all by Stephen Adly Guirgis.

Stacy Keach, perhaps best known for his award winning starring role in the pioneering TV series *Mike Hammer*, began his film debut in *The Heart is a Lonely Hunter*. His many other film credits include *The New Centurions*, *Fat City*, *Escape from L.A.*, *the Pathfinder*, *Up in Smoke*, *Hemingway*, *Intimate Strangers*, and the forthcoming *Honeydripper*. Recently he returned to television as the commanding father on the FOX sitcom *Titus*. His extensive work in film, TV, and theater, especially as a Shakespearean actor, and in such plays as *Deathtrap* and *The King and I*, has awarded him many honors, including Golden Globe, Emmy, and Tony Award nominations. He is the narrator of numerous documentaries, radio shows, and books on tape, including the short stories of Ernest Hemingway, and was the director of such films as Arthur Miller's *Incident at Vichy*.

Swoosie Kurtz is an award-winning actress who has appeared in several television series including *Sisters*, *Pushing Daisies*, *Still Standing*, and *Lost*. She received an Emmy for her role in the comedy series *Carol & Company*, as well as Broadway's "triple crown"—Tony, Drama Desk, and Outer Critics Circle awards— for her performance in *The Fifth of July*. Her movie credits include *Bright Lights, Big City*, *Against All Odds*, *The World According to Garp*, and *Liar, Liar*.

Michael Lally has published twenty-seven books of poetry and prose, written and directed several plays and screenplays and acted in numerous movies, plays, and television programs such as *Deadwood* and *L.A. Law*. He has also won the American Book Award and the PEN Josephine Miles Award for Excellence in Literature.

Alix Lambert's documentary *The Mark of Cain* was nominated for an Independent Spirit Award and aired on *Nightline*. She is an editor-at-large and writer for "Stop Smiling" magazine and a contributing editor for the literary journal "Open City". Lambert is currently a writer and associate producer for HBO's *John From Cincinnati*.

John Landis rose to international recognition in 1978 as director of the wildly successful *Animal House*. With international blockbusters such as *The Blues Brothers*, *Trading Places*, *Spies Like Us*, *Three Amigos!* and *Coming to America*, Landis has directed some of the most popular film comedies of all time. Other feature credits include *Into the Night*, *Innocent Blood*, *Oscar*, and *The Stupids*. Landis also wrote and directed the 1981 horror genre classic, *An American Werewolf in London*, and collaborated with Michael Jackson to direct the ground-breaking music videos *Thriller* and *Black and White*. His recent work includes the independent film, *Slasher*, and the full-length documentary *Mr. Warmth, the Don Rickles Project*, and the producing/directing of such TV shows as *Dream On* and *Honey I Shrunk The Kids* via his production company, St. Clare Entertainment. The recipient of many awards, including the 2004 Time Machine Career Achievement Award at the Sitges Film Festival in Spain, his life and work will be the subject of a biography by Giulia D'Agnolo Vallan to be published by M Press Books in 2008.

Melissa Leo is best known for playing the tough-minded detective Kay Howard on the award-winning TV series *Homicide: Life on the Street*. Her early work in television won her an Emmy nomination for her role on *All My Children*. Leo's role as Benicio Del Toro's wife in *21 Grams* (2003) won her recognition from the L.A. Film Critics Association, who named Leo the runner-up for Best Supporting Actress. Recently she has appeared in the movies *Mr. Woodcock* and *The Three Burials of Melquiades Estrada*.

John Lithgow debuted on Broadway in 1973 in *The Changing Room*, receiving both a Tony and a Drama Desk Award. His work on Broadway continued with starring roles in *Requiem for a Heavyweight* and *M Butterfly*, for which he received Tony Award nominations and, most recently, in *Dirty Rotten Scoundrels*. He has also received acclaim for his work in such films as *The World According to Garp*, *Terms of Endearment*, *Blow Out*, *Kinsey*, and, most recently, *Dreamgirls*, receiving two Academy Award nominations, and in television, earning three Emmys for his starring role in NBC's *3rd Rock from the Sun*. He is also the best-selling children's book author of the series *Farkle and Friends*, among other books.

Billy Luther, producer and director, studied film at Hampshire College and worked for the Smithsonian Institution's National Museum of the American Indian-Film and Video Center. A past honoree of Film Independent's Project: Involve, Luther was recently selected for the 2006 Sundance Ford Fellowship, CPB/PBS Producers Academy at WGBH, and Tribeca Institute's All Access

Program with his feature documentary *Miss Navajo*, which world-premiered at the 2007 Sundance Film Festival and was the winner of Michael Moore's 2007 Special Founders Prize. He is in development on the documentaries *Grab* and *The Untitled Indian Marching Band Project*. Luther belongs to the Navajo, Hopi and Laguna Pueblo Tribes. More information can be found at www.missnavajomovie.com.

Peter MacNicol began his acting career in the play, *Crimes of the Heart* for which he won the Theatre World Award. His stage performances eventually led him to films such as *Sophie's Choice* and *Ghostbusters II*. MacNicol is best known among television viewers for his Emmy Award-winning role on *Ally McBeal* and he currently stars in the drama *NUMB3RS*. His upcoming work includes that of director and writer of the movie *Salvation on Sand Mountain*, and as an actor in the new Spider-Man series, *The Spectacular Spider-Man*.

Matthew Maher has appeared in a number of films and television shows, including, most recently, the film *Gone Baby Gone* and the HBO series *John From Cincinnati*. He has also appeared on stage extensively over the years, Off-Broadway, Off-Off Broadway and regionally, at The Public Theater, Playwrights Horizons, Theater for a New Audience, Soho Rep, The Foundry Theater, The Actors Studio, Berkeley Rep, and the Actors Theater of Louisville, among many others. He has received an Obie Award, a Joseph Jefferson Award Nomination, and is an Associate Artist of the Civilians, an award-winning New York company.

Walter Mosley is the author of 29 critically acclaimed books, two of which have been made into movies: *Devil in a Blue Dress* and *Always Outnumbered*. His short fiction and essays have appeared in magazines including *The New Yorker* and *GQ*, among others. Mosley is also the recipient of numerous honors, including a Grammy and the NAACP Award in Fiction.

Tim Blake Nelson has acted in over 35 films including *O Brother, Where Art Thou?*, *The Good Girl*, *Minority Report*, *Syriana*, and the critically-acclaimed HBO film, *Warm Springs*. He directed the film *"O"* based on Shakespeare's Othello, and wrote and directed *The Grey Zone*, based on his play by the same name. He is on the Board of Directors for The Actors Center in New York City, The Creative Coalition, as well as the Soho Repertory Theater.

Michael O'Keefe's first acclaimed film role, as the oldest son of a Marine aviator in *The Great Santini*, starring Robert Duvall, received a Best Supporting Actor Oscar nomination. He then starred as Danny Noonan in the comedy film *Caddyshack*. He recently appeared on Broadway as the lead (with Mary-Louise Parker) in Craig Lucas's award-winning play, *Reckless*, and in the movie *Michael Clayton*, starring George Clooney. His other film credits include *Ironweed*, *The Pledge*, and *American Inquisition*. Perhaps best known for his portrayal of Fred, the husband of Roseanne's sister Jackie, on the ABC series *Roseanne*, his additional television credits include appearances on *The West Wing*, *Saving Grace*, and five appearances on the *Law & Order* franchise. O'Keefe is a published poet, with a 2006 Master's Degree in Poetry from The Writing Seminars at Bennington College. He is also a practicing Zen Buddhist, and became a Zen priest in 1994. He helped to found the Black Mountain Zen Centre in Belfast, North Ireland.

Mary-Louise Parker currently stars on the acclaimed Showtime series *Weeds*, for which she has won both a Golden Globe Award and an Emmy Award. She made her Broadway debut in 1990 with Craig Lucas's *Prelude to a Kiss*, earning the Clarence Derwent Award and a Tony nomination. Parker's film credits include *The Client* (1994) and *The Five Senses* (1999), *Longtime Companion*, *Fried Green Tomatoes*, and *Let the Devil Wear Black*.

Kyra Sedgwick is currenly in her third season of *The Closer*, so far winning a Golden Globe Award, two consecutive Screen Actors Guild Award nominations, an Emmy nomination, and two Golden Satellite Awards. She recently co-starred and produced the independent film, *Loverboy*, with husband Kevin Bacon, as well as developed and produced *Cavedweller*, for which she received an Independent Spirit Award.

Paul Simon, the multi-Grammy awarding-winning international honored singer and songwriter, wrote the screenplay, and starred in the film, *One Trick Pony*. He has also worked as an actor in such films as *Panic Room* and *RobbyKallePaul*, and his music has provided award-winning soundtracks for numerous movies, most recently *Garden State*. He recently received the first Library of Congress Gershwin Prize for Popular Song.

Stewart Stern is an Academy Award-nominated screenwriter. He is best known for writing the 1955 film *Rebel Without A Cause*, starring James Dean; and *Sybil*. Stern currently teaches screenwriting classes at the University of Washington and The Filmschool. He is the subject of Jon Ward's documentary, *Going Through Splat: The Life and Work of Stewart Stern*.

David Strathairn is an award-winning actor and producer born in California. He most recently appeared in *The Spiderwick Chronicles* and *The Bourne Ultimatum*, and on the HBO series *The Sopranos*. His work has earned him multiple nominations, including a Best Actor Oscar Award Nomination for *Good Night, Good Luck*, an Independent Spirit Award, and a Volpi Cup award from the Venice Film Festival. His other movie credits include *L.A. Confidential*, *Eight Men Out*, *Passion Fish*, and *The Firm*, and the forthcoming *Hereafter* and *A Tale of Two Sisters*.

Holland Taylor, currently starring in the TV sitcom *Two and a Half Men*, began her film career with the movies *Bosom Buddies* and *Romancing the Stone*. Her other film credits include *The Truman Show*, *Spy Kids 2*, *To Die For*, and *The Jewel of the Nile*. Her recurring role on *The Practice* won her one of two Emmy nominations, and her performance on *The Lot* got her a nomination as well. She recently appeared in the movie *Legally Blonde*, as well as other televisions shows including *ER* and *Monk*, and starred in the theatrical production of *The Graduate*.

Lili Taylor currently stars in *State of Mind*, a new television series about therapists in group practice. Most recently she appeared in the films *The Notorious Betty Page* and *High Fidelity*. Taylor has received numerous awards for her film, television, and stage appearances, including two Emmy nominations, a Screen Actors Guild Award, and an Obie Award, among others.

Stanley Tucci is known for his work in films such as *Kiss of Death*, *Road to Perdition*, and *Big Night*, and in the television series *Murder One*. He has won two Golden Globes for separate HBO films, and an Emmy for a guest appearance on *Monk*. Tucci recently appeared as Chief of Emergency Medicine on the television medical drama *ER*.

Taika Waititi is a New Zealand-born writer, film director, and comedian. His short film *Two Cars, One Night* (2003) was nominated for an Academy Award, among other honors. In 2007 Waititi was named one of the Top 10 Directors to Watch by *Variety* magazine. His latest release is *Eagle vs. Shark* (2006), a romantic comedy.

George Wendt is an actor best-known for his role as Norm Peterson on the hit television series *Cheers*. His other TV and film credits include *Fletch*, *Airplane II*, *Never Say Die*, *Lakeboat*, and the forthcoming *House of Re-Animantor*, as well as the Michael Jackson video *Black and White*. Wendt, who is currently appearing in Broadway's *Hairspray*, spent several years performing onstage for Chicago's premier comedy group Second City before breaking onto the screen. His work has earned him six Emmy nominations, among many other awards.

Dianne Wiest first gained acclaim for her performance in *The Purple Rose of Cairo* (1985) and won an Oscar for her performance in *Hannah and Her Sisters* (1986). Wiest followed her Academy Award success with *The Lost Boys* (1987) and *Parenthood* (1989), for which she received an Oscar nomination. She won her second Oscar in 1994 with *Bullets Over Broadway*. She recently had a featured role on the TV series *Law & Order*, and her other movie credits include *I Am Sam, Edward Scissorhands*, and the forthcoming *Passengers, In Treatment*, and *Poe*.

Alfre Woodard has been nominated for an Academy Award and has won three SAG Awards and one Golden Globe Award. Woodard's television credits include *Hill Street Blues, L.A. Law*, the television movie *Miss Evers' Boys*, and *The Practice*, all gaining her four Primetime Emmy Awards. Woodard's role in ABC's *Desperate Housewives* earned her an Emmy nomination as well. She will soon appear in the films *Bury Me Standing, American Inquisition*, and *The Family That Plays Together*, among others.

ABOUT THE EDITOR

JASON SHINDER

Jason Shinder's recent poetry books are *Among Women* and *Arrow Breaking Apart*. A recipient of 2007 poetry fellowships from the National Endowment for the Arts and the Massachusetts Council on the Arts, his poetry has appeared in the *New Yorker*, *Paris Review*, and elsewhere. His other books include *Best American Movie Writing*; *Writers on Therapy*, and *The Poem That Changed America; "Howl" Fifty Years Later*. He is the founder/director of the YMCA National Writer's Voice, YMCA Arts & Humanities, and the Gibson Music International Program, and teaches in the graduate writing program at Bennington College. His work within the filmmaking community has included directing the Arts Writing Program at Sundance Institute. He lives in New York and Massachusetts.

ACKNOWLEDGEMENTS

Many people helped in making *The Poem I Turn To* the first anthology to present poems that have inspired many of today's most distinguished actors, directors, and movie makers.

Chief among them are those without whom the book could not have happened – the contributors. Thanks to each and every one for responding so generously and thoughtfully. Your support and interest in the place poetry has in our lives was passionate and inspiring.

The book's advisory editors, Michael O'Keefe and Lili Taylor, were also, of course, essential to the book taking shape. Thank you. As actors they reached out to their friends but, also, and more importantly, provided a hands-on, sustained understanding of the constants and changes of the art of movie-making and its community.

Although not officially an advisory editor, Carol Muske-Dukes, the poet, fiction writer, and essayist, played an utterly critical role throughout the development of the book. It is her late husband, the actor David Coleman Dukes, for whom the book was, in part, conceived—as a way to remember him and to support The David Coleman Dukes Memorial Theater Scholarship Fund at the University of Southern California. On this note, many thanks to Madeline Puzo, Dean of the USC School of Theatre, for her valuable support and suggestions regarding the book's content and context.

The assistants of many of the book's contributors provided critical information and other sources of support. Many thanks to Chris Close, Amy Cutter, Elizabeth Czander, Amy Guenther, Karen Goldstein, Tony Montenieri, Les Peters, and Whitney Tancred.

I am also grateful to the many people who suggested actors or movie-makers to contact, and/or contacted them on their own. Thanks to Sophie Cabot Black, Philip Himberg, Donna Masini, Honor Moore, Elise Paschen, Bird Runningwater, and Liam Rector.

We were very fortunate to have the ample support of Tree Swenson, the Executive Director of The Academy of American Poets. Among many other services and activities, the academy is the headquarters of our country's annual National Poetry Month each April. Tree, and her office, provided ongoing input and encouragement, as well as special access to their website for biographical and other information.

We were also very fortunate to have the Grammy award-winning musician and producer, Diane Scanlon, oversee the production of the CD. Thanks to Diane. And thanks also to the many studios and engineers/owners that provided invaluable services, including Charles de Montebello at CDM Sound Studios in New York City; Jack Connors at Interlochen Public Radio Station in Interlochen, Michigan; Jerry Maybrook at The Media Staff in Los Angeles, California; Jean at Warrenwood Sound Studios in Los Angeles, California, and the Bad Animal Studios in Seattle, Washington.

Thanks to Fred Courtright and his company for their work on securing permissions to reprint the poems. Thanks, too, to the many photographers of the photos in the book, the list of credits of which are printed elsewhere in this book.

Alex Smithline and Phyllis Westberg, agents at Harold Ober Associates, helped shape the book's original and ongoing direction. Todd Green, editor at Sourcebooks MediaFusion, provided ongoing, patient, and invaluable editorial input and work. Thank you. My gratitude also to Dominique Raccah and Todd Stocke at Sourcebooks for their assistance and support.

Finally, my gratitude to the poet Cynthia Lowen who provided much-needed and timely research and editorial assistance.

The book offers a new community of poets, actors, directors, and other movie-makers. Steven Bauer, Sophie Cabot Black, Lucie Brock-Broido, Victoria Clausi, Tony Hoagland, Marie Howe, Elise Paschen, Askold Melnyczuk, Carol Muske-Dukes, Liz Rosenberg, and Tree Swenson are part of my ongoing community who provide unswerving faith, support, love, and guidance. My deepest gratitude. Love also to Inan, Fiona, Jamie, Jennah, Jordan, Roan, Martin, and Nina.

POEM CREDITS

Anna Akhmatova, "Epilogue" from "Requiem" from *Poems of Akhmatova*, translated by Stanley Kunitz and Max Hayward. Copyright © 1973 by Stanley Kunitz and Max Hayward. Reprinted with the permission of Darhansoff Verrill Feldman Literary Agents. **Maya Angelou**, excerpt from "On the Pulse of Morning" from *The Complete Collected Poems of Maya Angelou*. Copyright © 1993 by Maya Angelou. Reprinted with the permission of Random House, Inc. **W. H. Auden**, "A Summer Night" from *W. H. Auden: Collected Poems*, edited by Edward Mendelson. Copyright © 1937 by W. H. Auden. Copyright © 1976 by Edward Mendelson, William Meredith, and Monroe K. Spears. Reprinted with the permission of Random House, Inc. and Faber and Faber, Ltd. **Gwendolyn Brooks**, "Love Song of Satin-Legs Smith." Reprinted by Consent of Brooks Permissions. **Charles Causley**, "I Am the Great Sun (Norman Crucifix of 1632)" from *Collected Poems*. Reprinted with the permission of David Higham Associates, Ltd. **Constantine Cavafy**, "In Despair" translated by Daniel Mendelsohn. Reprinted with the permission of the translator. **Paul Celan**, "Death Fugue" from *Poems of Paul Celan*, translated by Michael Hamburger. Translation copyright © 1972, 1980, 1988, 1994, 2002 by Michael Hamburger. Used by the permission of Persea Books and Anvil Press Poetry, Ltd. **E. E. Cummings**, "anyone lived in a pretty how town" and "i like my body when it is with you" from *Complete Poems 1904-1962*, edited by George J. Firmage. 1923, 1925, 1940, 1951, 1953, © 1968, 1991 by the Trustees for the E. E. Cummings Trust. Copyright © 1976 by George James Firmage Reprinted with the permission of Liveright Publishing Corporation. **Sunny Dooley**, "White Shell Ever-Changing Woman." Reprinted by permission. **Oriah Mountain Dreamer**, "The Invitation" from *The Invitation*. Copyright © 1995, 1999 by Oriah Mountain Dreamer. Used with the permission of HarperCollins Publishers. **T. S. Eliot**, excerpts from "East Coker" from *Four Quartets* from *T. S. Eliot: The Complete Poems and Plays 1909-1950*. Copyright 1940 by T. S. Eliot and renewed © 1968 by Esme Valerie Eliot. Reprinted with the permission of Harcourt, Inc. and Faber & Faber, Ltd. **Robert Frost**, "The Road Not Taken," "The Pasture," and "Forgive Oh Lord" from *The Poetry of Robert Frost*, edited by Edward Connery Lathem. Copyright 1916 and renewed 1944 by Robert Frost. Used by permission of Henry Holt and Company, LLC and Random House (UK) Ltd. **Nikki Giovanni**, "Ego Tripping" from *Re:Creation*. Copyright © 1973 by Nikki Giovanni. Reprinted with the permission of Broadside Press **Donald Hall**, "My Son, My Executioner" from *White Apples and the Taste of Stone: Selected Poems 1946-2006*. Copyright © 2006 by Donald Hall. Used by permission of Houghton Mifflin Company. All rights reserved. **Seamus Heaney**, "Casualty" from *Field Work*. Copyright © 1979 by Seamus

INDEX